Ellison's
French Menu Reader

For a quick translation of French menus

by Al Ellison

B.S. — Cornell University School of Hotel Administration
L.L.B. — Western Reserve University School of Law

Printed in U.S.A.

© Al Ellison 1977. All rights reserved including the translation into other languages. Reprints and other reproductions, even in sections, prohibited.

Al Ellison
1919 Purdy Ave.
Miami Beach, Fla. 33139

INTRODUCTION

One of the great misfortunes of travelling in Europe is "playing it safe" in the local restaurants. The "playing it safe" syndrome results from uncertainty in ordering that unfamiliar dish or from having once been disappointed. Since most waiters cannot translate the menu and written translations are hard to find, dining out in France can be a frustrating or uneventful experience.

Of course, if it were easy to translate the items on your menu, think of all the new adventures that await you. In answer to this overwhelming call for help, *Ellison's French Menu Reader* was created with the hungry and inquisitive travelers in mind.

This French Menu Reader provides the simplest means of translating a menu. It works just like a standard dictionary with each item alphabetically listed. In my *French Menu Reader* you will find a great number of popular items listed in as many ways as it would appear on the menu.

The only time you may disregard the first word is if it is the article THE (la, le, l', les). Generally the item will be listed under the second word, but you should check the L's first.

> *i.e.* **Le Caneton à l'Orange** (duck in orange sauce)
> if not listed under the L's, look up . . .
> **Caneton à l'Orange**

If the item is not quickly located in the book, this may be the result of one or two slight differences in words, therefore, skim the other listings under Caneton for the words that appear the most similar, or check the English section (Part II) to see what other words mean duck. Then look the dish up under this new word. Remember, in French, duck may be described by more than one word.

The words following the main item in the dish (Caneton) are usually descriptions of its preparation and side dishes and can be similarly attached to any main item such as chicken (Poulet) or veal (Veau). It is those words that may appear slightly different on each menu although they all mean the same thing.

On the occasion that you find a dish is not translated literally, this may happen when the word refers to a region of the country, a famous chef or a well-known celebrity and has no specific bearing on the meaning of the dish.

Except in the few situations described, you should have no trouble locating the translation of the different dishes. Remember, too, that most restaurants have menus listed out front so you can quickly choose what is most appealing before entering.

Now you can walk into any restaurant with confidence and quit "playing it safe."

I welcome any criticisms or suggestions you may have.

— *Al Ellison*

*To my mother and Uncle Maury
who have given me love and encouragement*

TABLE OF CONTENTS

Introduction

Section I — Dictionary of Menu Terms

Section II — My Favorite Foods — English to French

Section III — My Favorite Restaurants

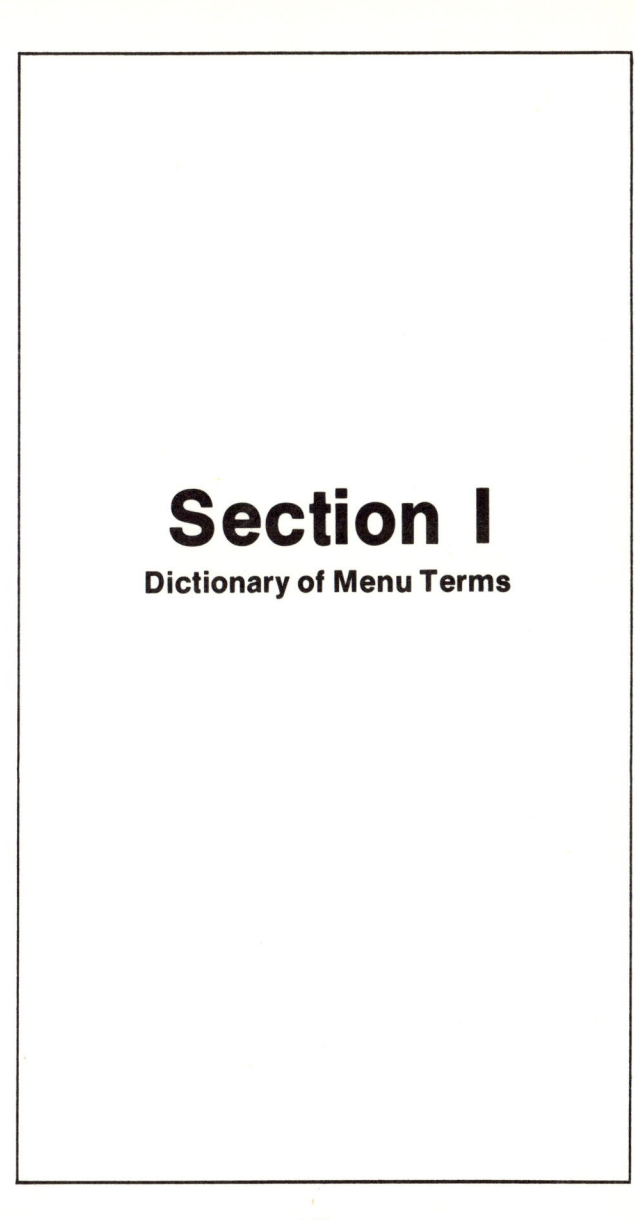

Section I
Dictionary of Menu Terms

Aigrefin

Abaisse: sheet of pastry
Abatis de Volaille: chicken giblets
Abats: from the head, tail, brain, tongue & entrails
Ablette: fish like carp
Abricot: apricot
Abricoter: to coat a cake with apricot jam
Abricots Bourdaloue: apricots, custard and almonds
Abricots Condé: apricots, vanilla syrup & sweet rice
Acarne: sea bream (fish)
Acave: fish similar to carp
Aceline: perch (fish)
Acétomel: syrup made of honey & vinegar
Adèle: Clear chicken broth
Adéline Patti: chicken broth with egg custard
Aeglé: tangelo (citrus fruit)
Africaine, à l': African style cooking
Agneau: lamb
Agneau à la Sauge: lamb cooked with sage
Agneau à l' Epée: lamb on a skewer
Agneau de Lait: baby lamb (milk fed lamb)
Agneau de Lait Landais: rack of baby lamb roasted with potatoes sautéed in goose fat
Agneau de Lait Persillé: grilled baby lamb & parsley
Agneau de Lait Rôti: roast baby lamb
Agneau de Pauillac: roast baby lamb
Agneau de Savournon: lamb from Savournon
Agneau des Alpilles Grillé sur Feu de Bois: lamb grilled over a wood fire
Agneau Grillé au Thym: broiled lamb with thyme
Agneau-Mouton: lamb
Agnes Sorel: cream, mushrooms & diced chicken soup
Agrousi: cucumber
Aïdo: roast shoulder of lamb with garlic
Aiglefin: fresh haddock
Aigo-boulido: soup with poached eggs
Aigo-saou: fish soup
Aigre de Cedre: citrus fruit
Aigre-Doux: sweet and sour sauce
Aigrefin: variation of aiglefin (haddock)
Aigrefin à la Crème: haddock with cream sauce
Aigrefin à la Flamande: haddock poached in white wine, onions & mushrooms

Aigrefin

Aigrefin à la Lyonnaise: haddock filets fried with onions
Aigrefin à la Portugaise: haddock baked with onions, garlic, tomatoes, rice and white wine
Aigrefin au Beurre: haddock with melted butter
Aigrefin aux Fines Herbes: poached haddock cutlets with white wine sauce
Aigrefin Fumé: smoked haddock
Aigrefin St. Nazaire: haddock cutlets with oysters, lobster slices and white wine sauce
Aigrette: light and flaky biscuits
Aiguillat: fish similar to catfish
Aiguillette de Barbarie au Cidre: roast rump of beef cooked with cider
Aiguillette de Boeuf: rump cut of beef
Aiguillette de Canard: duck breasts with cherries
Aiguillette de Canard à l'Aigre-Doux: duck breasts in a sweet & sour sauce
Aiguillette de Caneton: slices of duck in wine
Aiguillette de Poularde St. Albin: chicken with cream sauce, hard boiled eggs & ox tongue in aspic
Aiguillette de Rouennais à l'Orange: strips of duck breast with orange sauce
Aiguillette de Rouennais aux Cerises: strips of duck breast with cherries
Ail: garlic
Aile de Poulet: wing of chicken
Aile d'Oie au Sang: goose wings cooked in blood
Ailerons de Volaille à la Charcuterie: grilled chicken wings with pork sausage dipped in egg & bread crumbs
Ailerons de Volaille d'Uzes: boned chicken wings with pork forcemeat, wine, truffles & kidneys
Aillada: grilled snails, chives & leek sauce
Aillade: garlic is used
Aillade de Levraut: roast young hare with garlic
Aillade Toulousaine: walnut & garlic sauce
Aioli: garlic mayonnaise sauce
Airelles: cranberries
Aisy Cendré: cow's milk cheese
Albert: horseradish sauce
Albertine: poached fish with white wine
Albigensian Soup: soup from calf's feet, goose sausage & vegetables
Albigeoise: garnish for meat of stuffed tomatoes & potato croquettes

Aloyau

Albion: fish soup with lobster
Albran: very young duck
Alcide: white wine sauce with shallots & horseradish
Alevin: type of salmon
Alewife: fish of the herring family
Aligot: mashed potatoes with cream, butter, garlic & soft cheese
Alkekenge (Alcacange): strawberry
Allemande: white sauce with egg yolks, cream & meat juices or sautéed calf's kidneys, sweet peppers, onions & wine or clear beef broth with dumplings or beef broth with red cabbage & frankfurters
Allumettes: puff pastry with forcemeat or purée
Allumettes Glacées: puff pastry with egg whites & powdered sugar
Allumettes St. Hubert: puff pastry with game forcemeat and mushrooms
Alose: shad (fish)
Alose au Beurre Blanc: shad with whipped butter
Alose Oeufs d'Alose: shad (fish) roe (eggs)
Alouette: lark (fowl)
Alouette à la Bonne Femme: roast lark with bacon, croutons & brandy
Alouette à la Méridionale: lark with veal forcemeat & truffle sauce
Alouette à l'Anglaise: lark in egg & bread crumbs roasted
Alouette à la Normande: baked apple with lark
Alouette à la Paysanne: lark with bacon, onions and potatoes
Alouette à la Provençale: roast lark with sautéed mushrooms, olives, tomatoes, garlic & white wine
Alouette à la Turque: lark with onions, rice & eggplant
Alouette aux Olives: lark in butter, wine & olives
Alouette du Père Philippe: baked lark with bacon & potatoes
Aloyau: long strip around the loin
Aloyau de Boeuf: sirloin of beef
Aloyau de Boeuf à la Bretonne: beef sirloin roasted with lima beans
Aloyau de Boeuf à la Florentine: roast sirloin of beef, spinach, croquettes & brown sauce
Aloyau de Boeuf à la Lorraine: roast sirloin of beef, red cabbage, red wine, berries, potatoes & horseradish sauce
Aloyau de Boeuf à la Mode de Quimperle: Sirloin of beef, cider, brown sauce & lima beans

Aloyau

Aloyau de Boeuf à la Nivernaise: sirloin of beef with carrots & onions
Aloyau de Boeuf aux Céleris: roast sirloin of beef with brown sauce & celery
Aloyau de Boeuf aux Primeurs: roast sirloin of beef with vegetables & meat gravy
Amande: almond
Amande Amère: bitter almond
Amande Beurre: sweet almond
Américaine, à l': seafood sauce of brandy, tomatoes & white wine
Amoricaine, à l': seafood sauce of brandy, tomatoes & white wine
Amourettes: spinal marrow
Amourettes à la Française: beef marrow with mushrooms, white wine, vinegar & shallot butter
Amourettes à la Génoise: beef marrow with ham, rice & tomato sauce
Amourettes à la Sauce Câpres: beef marrow in hot caper sauce
Ananas: pineapple
Ananas à l'Orange: pineapple with oranges
Ananas Arrosée: pineapple with white liqueur
Ananas au Kirsch: pineapple with Kirsch
Ananas au Maraschino ou Kirsch: pineapple with cherry liqueur
Ananas Flambé: pineapple served flaming
Ananas Frais au Kirsch: pineapple with Kirsch
Ananas Tropical: tropical pineapple
Anchoiade: anchovy paste with oil on fried bread, onions & hard boiled eggs
Anchois: anchovy
Anchois à la Basque: anchovies fried in eggs & bread crumbs with tomatoes
Anchois à la Nicoise: boned anchovies with forcemeat & white wine
Anchois au Beurre: anchovy filets with butter & bread
Andalouse: tomatoes & mayonnaise
Andouille: smoked sausage from pork
Andouille de Guemené: large sausage from pork intestines & pork fat
Andouille de Vire: seasoned smoked pork sausage
Andouilles Vigneronne: chitterlings, salt pork & pig's tail with white beans, & white wine

Artichauts

Andouillette: grilled country sausage
Andouillette au Beaujolais Blanc: pork & beef sausage in white wine
Andouillette au Maison: small sausage with wine
Andouillette de Brochet: small sausage from pike meat
Andouillette de Chenas: small sausage of pork & chitterlings
Andouillette de Troyes: sausage from veal or pork tripe
Andouillette Flambée au Genièvre: sausage of pork chitterlings, pork fat, poached & flamed with gin
Andouillettes Grillées: sausage grilled & served with mustard
Anguille: eel
Anguille Fumée: smoked eel
Anguilles au Vert: eels poached in bouillon
Anjou: game consommé with asparagus tips
Antoine: scrambled eggs, bacon, & capers
Antoinette: poached fish in herb sauce
Apéritif: before dinner drink
A Point: rare (meat)
Appétit: appetite
Arachide: peanut
Araignée: hard shelled crab
Arapé: shell fish
Archidwchesse, à l': scrambled egg with ham & mushrooms
Arrigny: cow's milk cheese
Arlésienne, à la: soup from puréed kidney beans, white sauce & tapioca
Artichaut: artichoke
Artichaut à la Boulangère: artichoke filled pork forcemeat in pie dough
Artichaut à la Bréssane: artichoke with chicken forcemeat, bacon & white wine
Artichaut à l' Américaine: artichoke filled with chicken ragout, ox tongue, truffles & Américaine sauce (brandy, white wine, tomatoes)
Artichauts à la Grecque: artichokes in tomato & garlic
Artichauts à la Paysanne: artichokes with diced bacon, onions & potatoes
Artichauts à la Poivrade: artichokes with vinaigrette sauce, shallots & pepper corns
Artichauts à la Provençale: artichokes with green peas & lettuce

Artichauts

Artichauts à la Vinaigrette: artichokes in oil and vinegar dressing
Artichauts Foie Gras: artichokes with goose liver
Artichauts Vinaigrette: artichokes with oil & vinegar
Asperges: asparagus
Asperges à la Bernoise: asparagus with Swiss cheese, onions, bread crumbs & butter
Asperges à la Crème: creamed asparagus tips
Asperges à la Fribourgeoise: asparagus tips with Swiss cheese & butter
Asperges à l'Anglaise: asparagus tips on toast with egg yolk & butter sauce
Asperges à l'Espagnole: poached asparagus tips with vinaigrette sauce
Asperges à l'Italienne: baked asparagus tips with Parmesan cheese & butter
Asperges au Beurre: buttered asparagus
Asperges aux Fines Herbes: white asparagus tips with herbs
Asperges aux Carottes et Petits Pois: white asparagus with carrots & peas in German sauce (white wine, mushroom essence, lemon juice & egg yolks)
Asperges aux Morilles: asparagus tips with mushrooms
Asperges Colbert: asparagus tips on toast, Hollandaise sauce, whipped cream & poached egg
Asperges de Vineuil: variety of asparagus
Asperges de Pays au Jambon: asparagus & ham
Asperges Mornay: asparagus with grated cheese, creamy cheese sauce & butter
Asperges Mousseline ou Vinaigrette: asparagus with hot mousseline sauce (egg yolks, cream, whipping cream & lemon juice) or oil & vinegar dressing
Asperges Villeroi: white asparagus tips with truffle & ham sauce
Asperges Vinaigrette: asparagus with oil & vinegar dressing
Assiette Anglaise: cold assorted meats
Assiette Auvergnate (Jambon Cuit-Cru, Saucisson, Saucisse Sèche): dish of cooked & raw sausage and salami
Assiette de Charcuterie: plate of various sausages
Assiette de Cochonailles: pig's tails, backbones & head with pickles
Assiette de Crudités: vegetables with oil & vinegar dressing
Assiette de Hors d'Oeuvres: plate of hors d'oeuvres
Assiette de Hors d'Oeuvres Métropole: assorted appetizers

Aulagnier

Assiette de Salamis: plate of various salamis
Assiette des Viandes Froides: plate of cold cuts
Assiette Jambon de Paris: ham with French bread & butter
Assiette Jambon de Pays: ham with French bread & butter
Attereaux: skewered vegetables or meats in sauce
Auber, d': garnish for steaks
Auberge: country inn
Aubergine: eggplant
Aubergines à la Creme: eggplant in cream sauce
Aubergines à la Grecque: eggplant in white wine, oil, vinegar, onions, garlic, & licorice flavored herb
Aubergines à la Lyonnaise: fried eggplant with onions, bread crumbs & butter
Aubergines à l'Américaine: fried eggplant with mutton, rice, tomatoes, butter & garlic
Aubergines à la Mexicaine: eggplant with onions, tomatoes, green peppers, garlic & butter
Aubergines à la Napolitaine: eggplant with tomato sauce, Parmesan cheese & bread crumbs
Aubergines à l'Andalouse: fried eggplant with tomatoes, red peppers, ham & brown sauce
Aubergines à la Nicoise: eggplant with tomatoes & garlic
Aubergines à la Nimoise: eggplant in oil, red peppers, tomatoes, lemon juice & garlic
Aubergines à la Parisienne: eggplant with ham, lamb, ox marrow & onions
Aubergines à la Parmésan: eggplant with Parmesan cheese
Aubergines à la Roumaine: eggplant with tomatoes, rice cooked in tomato purée & lemon juice
Aubergines à l'Orientale: fried eggplant with onions, red peppers, mutton, rice, garlic & grated cheese
Aubergines au Four: fried eggplant with mutton, tomatoes, garlic & bread crumbs
Aubergines au Gratin: fried eggplant with bread crumbs & grated cheese
Aubergines Farcies: stuffed eggplant
Aubergines Frites à la Turque: fried eggplant with garlic
Aubergines Soufflées: fried eggplant with white sauce
Au Beurre d'Anchois: butter creamed with anchovies
Au Cerises: with cherry brandy or with cherries
Au Curaçao: with orange liqueur
Augusta, d': garnish for fish in white wine
Au Kirsch: with Kirsch (cherry liqueur)
Aulagnier: clear beef soup

Au Marasquin

Au Marasquin: with Maraschino liqueur
Au Poivre: with pepper corns
Auriol: mackerel
Autun: cheese
Aux Aromates: rich cream sauce
Aux Poireaux: with leeks
Auvergnate: pig's head soup
Avalanche des Hors d'Oeuvres: many different hors d'oeuvres
Avocat aux Crevettes: avocado with shrimp
Avocat en Saison: avocado in season
Avocat Farci de Crevettes: avocado stuffed with shrimp
Avocat Vinaigrette: avocado with oil & vinegar dressing
Baba: French cake
Baba au Rhum: sponge cake soaked in rum
Baba aux Marrons de l'Ardèche: sponge cake with rum & chestnuts
Babas: sponge cakes with raisins
Bacon: bacon or Canadian bacon
Baechkoffe: pork & lamb stew with vegetables
Bagration Salad: artichoke bottoms, celery, macaroni, mayonnaise & tomato purée with hard boiled eggs & truffles
Baguette: long French bread
Baies de Ronce Astoria: scooped apple in syrup, lemon juice, apricot jam, roasted almonds, blackberries & Kirsch apricot sauce
Baiser: 2 meringues with cream or jelly
Bajaina: small garden snail
Baleine: whale
Baliste: triggerfish
Ballotine: boned stuffed meat, foul, game or fish
Ballotine de Canard: roasted stuffed boned duck
Ballotine de Canard à la Fine Champagne: stuffed duck with cognac
Ballotine de Canard aux Girolles: stuffed duck with mushrooms in aspic
Ballotine de Canard Truffée au Foie Gras: poached duck with truffled goose liver & duck meat
Ballotine de Caneton aux Noisettes: stuffed duckling with hazelnuts
Ballotine de Dinde Truffée: boned turkey with chopped meat, pork and truffles
Ballotine de Lapin à l'Auvergnate: stuffed rabbit with lentils, leeks, potatoes and strips of pig's head meat

Barbe-de-Capucin

Ballotine de Pintadeau au Poivre Vert: boned stuffed hen with green peppers

Ballotine de Volaille à la Niçoise: boned chicken legs with forcemeat in white wine, onions, garlic, tomatoes & brown sauce

Ballotine de Volaille à la Princesse: boned chicken legs with forcemeat, truffles & potato croquettes

Ballotine de Volaille à l'Italienne: boned chicken legs with forcemeat & mushrooms in Italian sauce

Ballotine de Volaille aux Fines Herbes: boned chicken legs with forcemeat, white wine, tarragon & brown sauce

Ballotine de Volaille aux Pistaches: boned stuffed chicken with pistachios

Bambelle: fish of the carp family

Banane à la Crème Chantilly: banana with sugar & whipped cream

Banane à la Hôtelerie: banana with liqueur

Banane à la Niçoise: bananas with liqueur

Banane a l'Orientale: banana in lemon syrup with rose water, almond rice, whipped cream & almonds

Banane aux Fraises: banana with wild strawberries, sugar, orange liqueur & pistachios

Banane Bavarois: bananas with sugar, lemon juice, brandy & whipped cream

Banane Chinois: banana ice cream with ginger & whipped cream

Banane Meringuée: banana on vanilla rice with apricot sauce and meringues

Banane Meringuée au Chocolat: banana on vanilla rice with apricot sauce, meringues & chocolate

Bananes: bananas

Bananes au Cointreau: sliced bananas with liqueur

Bananes Créole: banana in rum on vanilla rice, crushed macaroons & sugar with apricot sauce

Bananes Flambées: bananas flamed with rum

Bananes Meunière: bananas sautéed in butter with lemon juice

Banane Split: banana split

Banquière, à la: tomato purée, butter, veal glaze and wine

Bar: ocean sea bass

Bar à l'Angevine: sea bass

Bar au Fenouil: sea bass with fennel (licorice herb)

Barbarin: fish of the mullet family

Barbe-de-Capucin: wild endive (chicory)

Barbel

Barbel: fresh water fish
Barbel à la Bourguignonne: fish in red wine with mushrooms & butter
Barbel à la Dijonnaise: fish in stock, butter, shallots, cream & mustard
Barbel à la Mentonnaise: fish with pike forcemeat, butter & white wine
Barbel à la Meunière: fried floured fish
Barbel à la Niçoise: baked fish with tomatoes, garlic, tarragon, anchovy filets, olives, lemon slices, capers & brown butter
Barbel à la Provençale: fish with garlic, tomatoes & oil
Barbel à la Ravigote: fish dipped in egg, bread crumbs & fried with ravigote sauce (white wine, tarragon vinegar, shallots, butter & chives)
Barbel à la Russe: fish in white wine butter, celery & chervil
Barbel à la Toulonnaise: fish with forcemeat & mussel sauce
Barbel au Gratin: fish with bread crumbs & grated cheese
Barbel au Raifort: fish fried with egg & bread crumbs with horseradish sauce
Barbel au Vin Blanc: fish in white wine
Barbel Frit: fish fried with egg, bread crumbs & tartar sauce
Barbel Masséna: fish with white wine, anchovy butter, lobster, mushrooms, mussels & brown sauce
Barbel Mirabeau: baked fish larded with anchovy filets
Barbel St. Charles: fish in white wine, butter with truffles, lobster & lobster eggs
Bar Beurre Rouge: bass with shellfish in butter
Bar Braisé au Champagne: bass braised with champagne
Barbue: brill (fish)
Barbue à la Bonne Femme: buttered brill filets, mushrooms, shallots & white wine
Barbue à la Boulonnaise: buttered brill pieces & mussels
Barbue à la Cancalaise: brill filets in white wine, oysters, shrimp, mushroom, cream & oyster sauce
Barbue à la Dieppoise: brill filets in white wine, mussels & shrimp
Barbue à la Française: brill pieces with Béarnaise sauce & tomato purée
Barbue à la Hyéroise: brill with forcemeat, white wine, butter, leeks, onions, egg yolks & cream
Barbue à la Marnière: brill filets in white wine with mussels & shrimp
Barbue à l'Amiral: brill in bouillon with wine, lobster butter,

Barbue

oysters, mussels, truffles & mushrooms

Barbue à la Normande: brill filets in white wine with oysters, mussels, mushrooms, truffles, shrimp, smelts, crayfish & Normande sauce (mushroom, oyster, egg & cream sauce)

Barbue à la Portugaise: brill filets with tomatoes, mushrooms & white wine sauce

Barbue à la Provençale: brill filets in white wine & oil with garlic, tomatoes, parsley, Provençale sauce (tomato & garlic sauce)

Barbue à la Régence: brill in white wine with poached oysters, mushrooms, truffles, carp roe (eggs), dumplings & crayfish

Barbue à la Riche: brill filets in white wine, crayfish tails, truffles & white sauce with cream & crayfish butter

Barbue à la Russe: brill filets with carrots, onions & lemon butter

Barbue à la Tyrolienne: brill filets with onions, tomatoes & white wine sauce

Barbue au Sauce Homard: brill with lobster sauce

Barbue Balmoral: brill cutlets in champagne with shallots, potatoes, spinach & crayfish tails

Barbue Bercy: brill filets with shallots, white wine, butter & lemon juice

Barbue Bonnefoy: brill pieces in butter & wine sauce

Barbue Chauchat: brill filets with boiled potatoes & cheese sauce

Barbue Donier: brill in white wine with risotto, creamy cheese sauce, grated cheese, butter & crayfish sauce

Barbue Duglère: brill in white cream wine sauce, butter, tomatoes & lemon

Barbue Grand Duc: brill filets in white wine, mushrooms, truffles, crayfish tails, asparagus tips & grated cheese

Barbue Madelaine: brill filets with forcemeat in white wine with tomato purée

Barbue Mantua: brill filets with forcemeat & mushrooms, white wine & Italian sauce

Barbue Montreuil: brill filets in white wine, potato balls & shrimp sauce

Barbue Mornay: brill filets, white wine, grated cheese & creamy cheese sauce

Barbue Rosine: brill filets in white wine, tomato purée & forcemeat

Barbue St. Germain: brill filets fried in bread crumbs with potato balls & Béarnaise sauce

Barbue

Barbue Wellington: brill filets in onion purée, grated cheese & white wine sauce & onion sauce
Bar en Croûte: bass cooked in a pastry shell
Barge: game bird prepared like a woodcock
Bar Grillé: grilled bass
Bar Grillé au Fenouil: grilled bass with fennel (licorice herb)
Barigoule: mushroom
Barigoule, à la: stuffed with mushrooms
Bar-le Duc: preserve made of currants
Baron d'Agneau: roast lamb
Barquette: puff pastry filled with seafoods, meats or vegetables in sauces
Barquettes: puff pastry with various fillings
Barquettes à la Créole: fried pastry with rice, tomatoes, okra & allspice
Barquettes à la Diable: fried pastry with pieces of calf's head, crayfish tails, red wine sauce & pepper
Barquettes à la Florentine: fried pastry with spinach leaves sautéed in butter, cheese soufflé and anchovy paste
Barquettes à la Gauloise: fried pastry with cockscombs, kidneys, chicken forcemeat, ham & brown sauce
Barquettes à la Normande: fried pastry with mushrooms, crayfish, oysters & Normande sauce (mushroom, cream, egg yolk & oyster sauce)
Barquettes à l'Ostendaise: fried pastry with oysters, truffles & white sauce
Barquettes aux Laitance: fried pastry with fish roe (eggs), butter, lemon juice & mustard
Barquettes Choisy: fried pastry with sole, cream sauce, braised lettuce, mushrooms & creamy cheese sauce
Barquettes de Gibier à la Chevreuse: fried pastry with game purée & diced game
Barquettes de Jambon à la Chevreuse: fried pastry with ham & curry sauce
Barquettes de Volaille à la Chevreuse: fried pastry filled with chicken & German sauce (white wine, egg yolk, mushroom & lemon juice sauce)
Barquettes Diana: fried pastry with game forcemeat, truffles, mushrooms & Diana sauce (pepper, cream, hard boiled egg whites & truffles)
Barquettes Mirabeau: fried pastry with sole purée, olives & anchovy butter
Barquettes Nantua: fried pastry with crayfish, butter, white sauce with crayfish butter & crayfish tails

Bavarois

Barquettes Régina: fried pastry with mushroom purée
Bartavelle: rock partridge (game bird)
Bar Truffé: bass stuffed with truffles
Baselle: like spinach
Basse Venaison: hare or rabbit meat
Bastardou: bird roasted like duck or goose
Bat: tail of a fish
Ba-ta-clan: pastry of almonds, eggs, vanilla & sugar
Bâtard: large French bread
Bâtarde Blonde: sauce made with fish fumet & white fish
Batelière, à la: garnish for fish consisting of mushrooms, onions, fried eggs & lobster
Bâton: long thin French bread
Bâtonnets: biscuits & pastries in the form of small sticks
Bâtonnets Royaux: fried hors d'oeuvres from pastry with minced chicken & partridge
Baudroie: anglerfish
Baudroie à l'Aïgo Sau: anglerfish & vegetable soup over garlic bread
Baudroie à la Nage: anglerfish in bouillon with herbs
Bavarois: dish made from custard, gelatine & whipped cream
Bavarois Adelhaide: orange flavored cream with wine
Bavarois à la Crème: custard pudding with whipped cream & coffee
Bavarois à la Diplomate: vanilla, chocolate & strawberry cream molds
Bavarois à la Florentine: almond cream with whipped cream flavored with liqueur & pistachios
Bavarois à la Religieuse: mold of chocolate & vanilla creams
Bavarois à la Vanille: vanilla cream mold
Bavarois à l'Espagnole: orange cream with orange pieces
Bavarois Alexandria: apricot cream with whipped cream & apricots
Bavarois à l'Impératrice: mold of wine jelly, cherries, vanilla cream & pistachios
Bavarois au Chocolat: chocolate cream mold
Bavarois aux Marrons: chestnut flavored cream
Bavarois Clermont: vanilla cream with chestnut purée & chestnuts
Bavarois Créole: vanilla cream with sweet rice, pineapple & whipped cream
Bavarois Dalmatienne: vanilla cream with sponge cake & Maraschino flavored fruit

Bavaroise

Bavaroise: garnish for fish of crayfish tails (lobster)
Bavarois Figaro: mold of creams & wine jelly
Bavarois Malakoff: vanilla cream with almonds, currants & lady fingers
Bavarois Marie Louise: peach cream with Kirsch liqueur
Bavarois Mocha: coffee flavored cream mold
Bavarois Praliné: vanilla cream with almond flavoring & nut bits
Bavarois Régine: vanilla & strawberry cream with soaked strawberries
Bavarois Richlieu: prune purée flavored with liqueur in vanilla cream
Bavarois Rubanée: layered almond, raspberry or strawberry & chocolate or coffee cream with wine jelly
Bavette: inner cut near loin of meat
Bavette Grillée Garnie: grilled steak of beef
Bayonnaise, à la: garnish for meat made of cooked macaroni in cream sauce
Béarnaise Sauce: sauce of wine, egg yolks, shallots & butter
Béatilles: tidbits
Beaufort: cheese similar to Swiss
Beaumont: cow's milk cheese
Beaupré de Roybon: cow's milk cheese
Bécada: woodcock & snipe (fowl)
Bécard: old salmon
Bécasse: woodcock (fowl)
Bécasse à la Bourguignonne: woodcocks roasted with brandy, red wine, onions, mushrooms & fried bacon
Bécasse à la Catalane: sautéed woodcock, shallots, bacon, garlic, sherry & brown sauce
Bécasse à la Riche: roast woodcock with liver purée & brandy
Bécasse à l'Ecaillière: woodcock with chopped chicken livers, oysters, bacon & entrails with paprika, sour cream, lemon juice & anchovy butter
Bécasse au Champagne: roast woodcock in champagne with pepper & lemon juice
Bécasse au Fine Champagne: woodcock roasted in cognac
Bécasse aux Truffes: woodcock with truffle sauce
Bécasse Carême: woodcock with brandy, mustard & lemon juice
Bécasse Cécilia: roast woodcock with game sauce & goose liver patty with aspic

Bel Paese

Bécasse en Papillote: woodcock roasted with onions, mushrooms, truffles & butter
Bécasse en Salmis: roasted woodcock with butter, mushrooms, shallots, & sherry
Bécasse en Salmis à la Chasseur: woodcock with mushrooms, white wine & brown sauce
Bécasse Favart: woodcock with goose liver forcemeat and truffles
Bécasse Flambée: woodcock roasted & flamed with cognac
Bécasse Flambée en Casserole: woodcock in casserole & flamed with brandy, chopped liver, entrails, lemon & cayenne pepper
Bécasse Lucullus: woodcock roasted with truffles, brown sauce, wine, kidney & dumplings
Bécasse Rôtie: roast woodcock with entrails, liver, watercress and lemon
Bécasse Rôtie à la Gascogne: woodcock roasted over vine cuttings
Bécasse Victoria: woodcock with goose liver, truffles, potatoes & brandy sauce
Bécassin: snipe (fowl) usually roasted
Beccaccia: woodcock & snipe
Bécessine en Casserole: snipe with bacon, butter & brandy
Béchamel: sauce of milk, butter & flour
Béhangue: broth of chicken with poached egg & chervil (licorice herb)
Beignet: fritter
Beignets d'Aubergines: eggplant fritters
Beignets de Brandade de Morue: fritters of puréed cod with milk, garlic & olive oil
Beignets de Fruits: fruit fritters
Beignets de Pommes: sugared apple fritters
Beignets Soufflés Flambés: flamed fritters with beaten egg whites
Belle-Chevreuse: variety of peach
Belle-et-Bonne: pear in red wine or syrup
Belle Hélène: garnish from mushrooms with tomato or green peas, young carrots & potato croquettes
Belons: oysters
Belons au Champagne: oysters cooked in champagne
Bel Paese: Italian cow's milk cheese

Bénédictine

Bénédictine: almond flavored sponge cake with liqueur & roasted almonds
Bercy: sauce of white wine, shallots & herbs in creamy butter
Bergamots: variety of pears
Berlingot: toffee with peppermint flavor
Bernard: hermit crab
Berny: mashed potatoes with truffles dipped in egg
Berrichonne: garnish of braised cabbage, chestnuts, bacon & little onions
Berro: watercress
Bertiche: perch
Bertines Mandelbann: apple meringue pie
Besi de Caissoy: pear
Besi de la Motte: pear
Bétises de Cambrai: mint flavored confection
Bette à la Crème: Swiss chard in cream sauce
Bette au Beurre: Swiss chard with butter
Bettes au Beurre ou Huile et Citron: buttered Swiss chard (vegetable) with oil & lemon
Bette au Gratin: Swiss chard with bread crumbs & grated cheese
Bette au Jus: Swiss chard in veal gravy & butter
Betteraves: beets
Betteraves à la Bordelaise: sautéed beets, onions & red wine sauce
Betteraves à la Crème: beets cooked in cream sauce
Betteraves à l'Américaine: beets in vinegar butter sauce
Betteraves à l'Ancienne: beets with onions in vinegar & butter sauce
Betteraves à la Paysanne: beets with onions & cream sauce
Betteraves à la Polonaise: beets with butter, vinegar & cloves
Betteraves à la Russe: beets with minted butter
Betteraves à la Sauce Moutarde: beets with vinegar & mustard sauce
Betteraves à l'Orange: beets in butter with orange sauce
Betteraves au Beurre: beets with onions & butter
Betteraves au Cumin: beets in vinegar with caraway seeds
Betteraves Epicées: beets with chopped onions, butter, sugar, cloves, vinegar & cinnamon
Betteraves et Céleri au Beurre: beets & celery in butter & onions
Betteraves Etuvées: beets stewed in butter
Betteraves Sautées: beets sautéed in butter

Blancmange

Beurre: butter
Beurré: pear dessert with liqueur
Beurre à l'Anglaise: melted butter
Beurre Arachides: peanut butter
Beurre, au: served with butter
Beurre Blanc: butter sauce with white wine
Beurre de Gascogne: sauce of garlic cloves, pork dumplings & butter
Beurre de Montpellier: butter dressing for cold dishes
Beurre Fondu: melted butter with lemon juice & herbs
Beurre Nantais: sauce of dry white wine, shallots, butter & seasonings
Beurre Noir: browned butter with vinegar
Beurre Noix: walnut butter
Bien Cuit: well cooked (meat)
Bière Bouteille: bottle of beer
Biftek: beefsteak
Biftek à Cheval: beef seasoned in hot butter
Biftek au Poivre: pepper steak
Biftek Sauté Bercy: beef steak with onions & butter sauce
Biftek Sauté Marchand de Vin: beef steak with wine sauce
Bigourade: orange sauce
Bigourades: bitter oranges
Bigorneaux: periwinkles (spiral sea mullusk) raw or boiled in seasoned water
Bijane: cold soup with crumbled bread & red wine
Billi Bi: cream of mussel soup
Biscuit de Brochet: pike biscuits (dumplings)
Biscuit de Reims: sweet dry biscuits
Biscuit Glacé: iced biscuits
Biset: rock pigeon
Bisque: milk or cream soup
Bisque de Crevettes: cream soup with shrimp
Bisque d'Ecrevisses Cardinal: crayfish cream soup with lobster roe (eggs)
Bisque de Homard: cream soup with lobster
Bisque de Homard Fine Champagne: cream soup with lobster & cognac
Bisque Soupe: cream soup
Blanchailles: whitebait (fish)
Blanchailles à la Diable: whitebait fried with pepper & lemon
Blanchailles à l'Indienne: whitebait fried with curry
Blanchailles Frites: fried whitebait
Blancmange: cold pudding made of almond, milk & gelatine

Blancmange

Blancmange à l'Anglaise: vanilla pudding
Blancmange au Cafe: coffee flavored pudding
Blancmange au Chocolat: chocolate flavored pudding
Blancmange au Maraschino: pudding with Maraschino liqueur
Blancmange aux Fraises: strawberry pudding
Blancmange aux Noisettes: hazelnut pudding
Blancmange aux Pistaches: pudding with pistachios
Blancmange Delmonico: pudding with cherry jam & cherries
Blancmange Rubane: chocolate, strawberry, vanilla & coffee puddings
Blanquette d'Agneau: lamb stew with onions, garlic, cloves & olive oil
Blanquette d'Agneau à l'Ancienne: stew with lamb, cream, onions & potatoes
Blanquette de Ris de Veau: veal sweetbreads stewed in white wine
Blanquette de Veau: creamed veal stew
Blanquette de Veau: poached veal with cream, onions & mushrooms
Blanquette Sauce: sauce of broth, egg yolk, cream & lemon
Blé Noir: buckwheat (cereal)
Bleu: blue cheese or very rare (for meat)
Bleu d'Auvergne: cow's milk cheese
Bleu de Basillac: blue cheese of the Roquefort type
Bleu de Bresse: creamy cheese
Bleu des Causses: rich sharp cheese
Bleu naturel de l'Aveyron: blue-veined cheese
Blinis: caviar filled pancakes with sour cream
Blinis au Saumon Fume: smoked salmon pancakes with sour cream
Bloc de Foie d'Oie Truffé: sharp goose liver pâté with truffles
Blond de Veau: concentrated veal broth
Blonde, Sauce: sauce used with meats & poultry
Boeuf: beef
Boeuf à la Bordelaise: beef sirloin in red wine with brown sauce
Boeuf à la Ficelle: filet of beef boiled in hot consommé
Boeuf à la Mode: rump roast of beef in pork fat with onions, brandy & white wine with herbs, spices, calf's feet & pig's trotters
Boeuf à la Mode aux Carottes: braised beef with wine & carrots
Boeuf aux Xérès: sautéed beef filet with sherry sauce

Boudin

Boeuf Bouilli: boiled beef
Boeuf Bouilli à la Bordelaise: beef slices sautéed with onion, garlic & white wine
Boeuf Bourguignon: beef with red wine, salt pork, onions & mushrooms
Boeuf en Daube: beef stew with red wine or beef stew with bacon, wine, herbs & vegetables
Boeuf Grillé au Fenouil: grilled steak with fennel (licorice herb)
Boeuf Gros Sel: boiled beef with vegetables in bouillon
Boeuf Gros Sel à la Ficelle: braised beef stew in bouillon
Boeuf Miroton: beef & onion stew
Boeuf Stroganoff: sliced beef in sour cream sauce
Boiedieu: chicken consommé
Boisson Non Compris: drink not included
Bombay Chicken: curried chicken on rice
Bombe: moulded ice cream
Bombe Alaska Flambée au Kirsch: baked Alaska served with cherry flavored liqueur
Bombes Glacées: ice cream in varying shapes with cream
Bonne Femme: mushrooms, onions & bacon garnish
Bordelaise: sauce made from red wine, shallots, thyme, bay leaf, pepper, meat glaze & butter with bone marrow
Bordure: ragout of various foods
Bordure à la Chasseur: ragout with partridge forcemeat, game dumplings, mushrooms, truffles & game sauce
Bordure a la Comtesse: ragout with chicken forcemeat, artichoke bottoms, asparagus tips & cream sauce with chicken & mushrooms
Bordure à la Parisienne: ragout with buttered rice, chicken livers, cockscombs, kidneys, mushrooms & brown sauce
Bordure à la Princesse: ragout with potatoes, chicken dumplings, asparagus tips, truffles & German sauce (white wine, mushrooms, lemon juice & egg yolk sauce)
Bordure à la Reine: ragout with truffles, chicken purée, rice, egg yolks & cream sauce
Borscht: beet soup
Bouchée Duchesse: mashed potato shell filled with mushrooms & truffle flavored creamed chicken
Bouchée Financière: pastry shells with chicken & lamb's brains in creamy truffle & sherry wine sauce
Bouchée à la Ficelle: bitesize servings of marrow
Bouchée à la Reine: chicken à la king in pastry
Boudin: blood sausage

Boudin

Boudin aux Châtaignes: pork blood sausage with chestnuts
Boudin Blanc: white sausage
Boudin de Campagne: blood sausage grilled & apple purée
Boudin Grillé Flamande: grilled blood sausage with purée of potatoes & apples
Boudin Noir aux Pommes: pork blood sausage with apples
Boudin Purée: purée of blood sausage
Bouillabaisse: seafood & fish soup
Bouillabaisse avec Langouste: seafood & fish soup with spiny lobsters
Bouillabaisse avec Rouille: seafood & fish soup with garlic, red peppers, oil, lobster coral (eggs) & pink sea urchin
Bouillabaisse du Pêcheur: fisherman's fish stew
Bouillabaisse Niçoise: fish soup/stew with tomatoes, fried garlic, capers, lemon juice, anchovy butter & black olives
Bouillinade des Pêcheurs: fish soup
Bouillon: broth of beef, chicken, game or fish with vegetables
Bouillon de Viande: meat broth
Boule de Neige: dessert with sauce of egg yolks & sugared cream or sponge cake with whipped cream
Bouquetière: garnish for meat consisting of baked potatoes, artichoke bottoms with turnips, carrots, beans, peas & cauliflower in Hollandaise sauce or vegetables arranged like flowers
Bouquets: red shrimp eaten cold & unpeeled
Bouquets Frits: butterfly jumbo shrimp
Bourride: fish soup with mayonnaise garlic sauce or fish stew with garlic & egg sauce
Bourride à la Rouille: fish stew with garlic sauce, olive oil, egg yolks, hot peppers, lobster coral (eggs) & pink sea urchin
Bourride avec Langouste: fish stew with spiny lobsters
Bourride "Ma Facon": fish soup with mayonnaise served on toast
Boursin: cheese flavored with garlic & chopped herbs
Braisé Chou: braised cabbage
Brandade de Morue: boiled cod, milk, garlic & olive oil with fried bread & truffles
Bréjauda: soup of cabbage, bacon & red wine
Brétonne: sauce of white wine, onion, tomato & garlic
Bric: dish of veal & lamb in pastry
Bricquebec: cheese from cow's milk
Brie: cheese from cow's milk
Brioche: cake of yeast dough, butter, flour & eggs or pâté in shape of a loaf

Brochette

Brioche de Foie Gras: goose liver pâté in a light cake
Brioche de Langouste au Porto: crawfish meat in a bread-like cake with port wine
Brioche Sauce Chocolat: yeast cake with chocolate sauce & whipped cream
Broche: spit
Brochet: pike (fish)
Brochet Beurre Blanc à l'Oseille: poached pike with whipped butter with chopped shallots sautéed in wine vinegar
Brochet Beurre Champenois: pike with a butter-cheese mixture
Brochet de Meuse: pike from the Meuse River
Brochet Rôti au Pouilly: pike baked in white wine
Brochette: skewer
Brochette à la Bohémienne: skewered ham, goose liver & truffles in paprika sauce
Brochette à la Financière: skewered cockscombs, kidneys, truffles, mushrooms & ham with brown sauce
Brochette à la Génevoise: skewered chicken liver, lamb sweetbreads, truffles, artichoke bottoms, ox marrow, tomato & garlic sauce
Brochette au Foies de Volaille: skewered chicken livers, mushrooms & bacon with herb butter
Brochette d'Agneau aux Herbes de Provence: skewered lamb with herbs
Brochette d'Agneau et Son Riz Compose: skewered lamb on rice
Brochette d'Agneau Provençale: skewered lamb with garlic & oil
Brochette de Filet de Boeuf aux Aromates: skewered beef filet with herbs
Brochette de Filet de Boeuf Vert Pré: skewered beef filet with crisp potatoes
Brochette de Fruits de Mer: skewered seafood
Brochette de Moules Sauce Tartare: skewered mussels with tartar sauce
Brochette de Rognons: skewered lamb kidneys with bacon, watercress & herb butter
Brochette de Rognons à l'Espagnole: skewered mutton kidneys, bacon & mushrooms with pepper
Brochette des Corsaires: assorted skewered seafood
Brochette des Gastronomes: items of gastronomical delight on skewers
Brochette de Volaille aux Poireaux: skewered chicken &

Brochette

leeks
Brochette Florida: skewered turkey, ham, pineapple & olives with orange butter
Brochette Lida: skewered calf's liver, sweetbreads, mushrooms & artichoke bottoms with melted butter
Brochette Pahlen: skewered lobster, oysters & mushrooms served on rice
Brochettes de Coquilles St. Jacques: broiled skewered scallops
Brochettes de Dinde: turkey chunks on a skewer
Brochettes de Langoustines: crawfish tails (lobster) broiled on skewer
Brochettes de Moules: mussels broiled on a skewer
Brochettes de St. Jacques Grillées: broiled scallops on a skewer
Brochettes Stucchi: skewered chicken liver, lamb sweetbreads, artichoke bottom, ham and truffles with tomato sauce
Brocoli: broccoli
Brocoli à la Lilloise: broccoli with onions & butter
Brocoli à la Romaine: broccoli fried with lemon slices
Brocoli à l'Italienne: broccoli with meat gravy & anchovy butter
Brocoli au Beurre: broccoli with butter
Brouet d'Anguilles: eel stew with ginger & pepper
Brouillade aux Truffes: scrambled eggs with truffles
Brouillé aux Tomates: scrambled eggs with tomatoes
Brunoise: soup of diced vegetables
Bucardes: cockles (shell fish)
Bûche de Noël: cake filled with butter, cream & various colored butter creams
Buffet Froid: assorted cold cuts with garnish
Cabillaud: fresh cod
Cabillaud à la Boulangère: cod with butter, potatoes, onions & garlic
Cabillaud à la Flamande: cod in white wine with shallots, herbs & lemon
Cabillaud à la Florentine: cod with spinach, cheese, butter & creamy cheese sauce
Cabillaud à la Génoise: cod in red wine, shallots, mushrooms & poached crayfish roe (eggs)
Cabillaud à la Maltaise: cod in white wine with shallots, anchovy butter, capers & herbs
Cabillaud à l'Andalouse: cod in white wine with tomato

Café

purée, red peppers & fried eggplant
Cabillaud à la Parisienne: cod in white wine, mushrooms & crayfish
Cabillaud à la Portugaise: cod with onions, garlic, tomatoes & white wine
Cabillaud à la Printanière: cod fried in butter, peas & potatoes
Cabillaud à la Reine: cod with forcemeat dumplings & cream sauce
Cabillaud à l'Espagnole: cod fried in oil with tomatoes, onions & red peppers
Cabillaud à l'Indienne: cod slices with curry sauce & rice
Cabillaud au Beurre d'Anchois: fried cod with anchovy butter
Cabillaud au Four: cod with salt pork, onions, potatoes & tomatoes
Cabillaud au Gratin: cod with bread crumbs & grated cheese
Cabillaud aux Champignons: cod with mushrooms, butter & lemon juice
Cabillaud aux Fines Herbes: cod with finely chopped herbs
Cabillaud aux Nouilles: cod with noodles in cream sauce
Cabillaud Bandong: cod in lemon juice with curry & shallots, fried in butter with rice, chutney & mushrooms
Cabillaud Bouilli: cod with capers, shrimp, anchovies, lobster & melted butter
Cabillaud Dimitri: cod with white wine sauce, anchovy filets & anchovy butter
Cabillaud Frit: cod dipped in egg & bread crumbs, fried in butter with tartar or tomato sauce
Cabillaud Halévy: cod with white wine sauce, shrimp sauce, truffles, lobster coral (eggs) & potatoes
Cabillaud Héloïse: cod with mushrooms & shallots in white wine
Cabinet, Pouding de: pudding from sponge cake (lady fingers) cooked in Kirsch or Maraschino with chopped fruit & raisins
Cabrion: goat's milk cheese
Cachat: goat's milk cheese with white vinegar
Café Américain: American coffee
Café au Lait: coffee with milk
Café Filtré: filtered or drip coffee
Café Glacé: coffee ice cream frozen in goblet with whipped cream

Café

Café Liègeois: coffee flavored mixture of eggs, sugar & cream cheese topped with whipped cream
Café Viennois: coffee with whipped cream
Caille: quail
Caille à la Berlinoise: boned quail with goose liver forcemeat & artichoke bottom with German sauce (white wine, mushroom, egg yolk & lemon juice sauce)
Caille à la Bohémienne: boned quail with goose liver & truffles with veal gravy
Caille à la Canadienne: roast quail with apples, red wine & brown sauce
Caille à la Charentaise: roast quail in vine leaves, bacon & cognac
Caille à la Crème: roast quail with cream sauce, meat glaze & lemon juice
Caille à la Dauphine: roast quail in baked potato with truffle sauce
Caille à la Liègeoise: quail roasted with berries & liqueur
Caille à la Milanaise: fried quail in egg & bread crumbs with grated cheese & devil sauce (white wine, pepper, shallots, vinegar & brown sauce)
Caille à l'Ananas: quail roasted with veal gravy, pineapple juice & diced pineapple
Caille à la Normande: baked apple filled with boned quail
Caille à la Princesse: boned quail with goose liver forcemeat & veal stock on asparagus tips
Caille à la Turque: quail braised in herb sauce
Caille à l'Egyptienne: roast quail on herbed rice & tomato sauce
Caille à l'Espagnole: quail in oil with green pepper, peas, tomatoes & garlic sausage
Caille Alexandria: quail in white stock with truffles, grated cheese, asparagus tips & creamy cheese sauce
Caille Alexis: quail roasted with liqueur, cream & raisins
Caille à l'Orientale: roast quail with tomato juice & veal gravy on saffron rice
Caille au Choucroute: quail in bacon & sauerkraut
Caille au Chou Rouge: roast quail on red cabbage with apple & chestnut purée
Caille au Malaga: quail roasted with wine veal gravy & raisins
Caille au Petit Duc: quail dipped in egg & bread crumbs with mushrooms with horseradish sauce
Caille aux Cerises: roast quail in brandy, lemon juice &

Cailles

cherries
Caille aux Coings: quail in brandy & quince (fruit), cooked in butter gravy with quince jelly
Caille aux Laitues: quail roast & lettuce
Caille aux Petits Pois: roast quail with peas & ham
Caille aux Raisins: quail in veal stock with grapes & white wine
Caille Carmen: quail in veal stock with white port wine
Caille Clermont: boned quail with chestnuts, butter, onions, & white wine sauce
Caille d'Amérique: American quail
Caille de Dombes en Cocotte aux Raisins: quail in a casserole with grapes
Caille Demidoff: braised quail with carrots, turnips, celery, onions & truffles
Caille Diana: roast quail with chestnut purée & Diana sauce (game dumplings, truffles & sherry sauce)
Caille en Croûte: quail baked in a pastry crust
Caille Figaro: quail with truffles, sausage & veal stock
Caille Fourrée au Foie Gras: quail stuffed with duck or goose liver
Caille Frères Provençaux: quail in butter & baked in puff pastry
Caille George Sand: quail with goose liver forcemeat & butter & baked in puff pastry
Caille Judic: quail on lettuce with kidneys, truffles & brown sauce
Caille Kléber: quail in pastry shell with mushrooms, goose liver & sauce
Caille Maintenon: quail with truffles, game forcemeat, truffles, mushrooms & truffle sauce
Caille Marianne: roast quail with apple slices, bread crumbs & butter
Caille Médicis: poached quail with goose liver, truffles, macaroni & wine sauce, game essense & butter
Caille Richelieu: boned quail with truffles, carrots, celery & onions
Caille Rôti au Nid: roast quail & artichoke bottoms with purée of chestnuts on top
Cailles à la Bonne Femme: quail casserole with butter, bacon, potatoes & carrots
Cailles aux Cerises: quails in butter with cherries
Cailles Sous la Cendre: quails with livers & forcemeat in

Caille

vine leaves all charcoal broiled
Caille Sur Canapé: quail on toasted triangles of bread
Caille Victoria: quail with goose liver, truffles with potatoes, brandy & veal gravy
Caillette aux Herbes Fines: young quail with finely chopped herbs
Caillette de l'Ardèche: baked quail with liver pâté
Cake Anglais: loaf style cake
Cake au Beurre: simple butter cake
Cake au Citron: pound cake flavored with lemon
Camembert: soft cheese made of cow's milk
Calmar: squid
Calmar à la Ménagère: fried squid with onions, tomatoes, saffron rice & fennel (licorice flavored herb)
Calmar Braisé: squid with white wine, butter, anchovies, garlic & tomato sauce
Calmar en Matelote: quail in oil with onions, garlic, tomatoes, white wine & mushrooms
Canapé d'Anchois: small toast with anchovies
Canapé de Caviar: small toast with caviar
Canapé de Champignons: small toast with mushrooms
Canapé de Crevettes: small toast with shrimp in Hollandaise sauce (Butter, egg yolk, cream & lemon sauce)
Canapé de Quenelle: dumpling on toast with creamy cheese sauce
Canard: duck
Canard à la Bordelaise: roast duck with bread pieces, chopped liver, olives & garlic
Canard à la Bourguignonne: duck in red wine, brown sauce, potatoes, onions & bacon
Canard à la Fermière: duck in white wine with carrots, turnips, celery, onions, green beans & peas
Canard à la Flamande: duck with cabbage, bacon, truffles, carrots, turnips & garlic sausage
Canard à la Gaston Godard: duck with dumplings made of mushrooms, ox tongue, cockscomb, kidneys, lamb sweetbreads & truffles with a creamy sauce
Canard à l'Alsacienne: duck on sauerkraut with potatoes & gravy
Canard à la Lyonnaise: duck with onions & chestnuts
Canard à la Maltaise: duck in white wine with bitter oranges
Canard à la Menthe: duck roasted in a casserole with veal gravy & mint

Canard

Canard à la Moderne: duck seasoned with butter & braised in wine with shallots & anchovies
Canard à l'Ancienne: duck on sauerkraut with bacon, sausage, carrots & gravy
Canard à l'Anglaise: duck with sage & onions stuffing
Canard à la Normande: duck with apple liqueur, cider, sour cream & apple pieces
Canard à la Provençale: duck pieces in white wine, tomatoes, garlic, anchovies, basil & black olives
Canard à la Royale: stuffed duck with duck liver & truffles
Canard à la Russe: braised duck with cucumbers & sour cream
Canard à l'Orange: duck with orange sauce
Canard à l'Orange Entier: whole duck in orange sauce
Canard au Chou: duck pieces with cabbage & bacon
Canard au Malaga: duck in onions & carrots in red wine
Canard au Muscadet: duck cooked with white wine
Canard au Poivre Vert: roast duck with green peppers
Canard aux Ananas: roast duck with pineapple
Canard aux Cerises: roast duck with cherries
Canard aux Concombres: duck with cucumbers & croutons with gravy
Canard aux Navets: duck in brown sauce with turnips
Canard aux Oignons: roast duck & onions with sugar
Canard aux Petits Pois: duck with peas, lettuce, bacon, onions & brown sauce
Canard aux Raisins: duck in red wine & veal gravy with orange peel & grapes
Canard Beaulieu: roast duck with olives, artichoke bottoms & sauce
Canard Bouilli: boiled duck & onions with horseradish or onion sauce
Canard de Barbarie en Ballotine: boned & steamed duck
Canard de Barbarie Rôti aux Olives: roast duck with olives
Canard de Challans à la Broche: duck roasted on a spit
Canard Duclair: duck with bread pieces, chopped liver, red wine & orange juice sauce
Canard en Crépinette: duck stuffed in a membrane
Canard Farci à l'Allemande: duck with apples, red cabbage, potatoes & gravy
Canard en Croûte d'Amiens: duck with bacon & duck liver with brandy
Canard Farci à l'Estragon: roast duck with tarragon
Canard Nantais aux Olives: roast duck with olives

Canard

Canard Rouennaise: duck with brandy sauce
Canard Sauvage: wild duck
Canard Sauvage au Suc d'Ananas: wild duck with pineapple juice & sugar
Caneton: duckling
Caneton à la Bigarade: duckling in orange sauce
Caneton à la Rouennaise: roast duckling with mustard, spices & red wine
Caneton à l'Orange: roast duckling with orange sauce
Caneton au Boudin: roast duckling with blood sausage
Caneton au Cidre: duckling with cider
Caneton au Poivre Vert: duckling with green pepper
Caneton aux Ananas: duckling served with pineapple
Caneton aux Cerises Flambé au Kirsch: flamed duckling with cherries & cherry liqueur
Caneton aux Navets et Petits Oignons: duckling with turnips & little onions
Caneton aux Olives: duckling with olives
Caneton aux Oranges: roast duckling with oranges
Caneton aux Pêches: duckling with peaches
Caneton aux Truffes: roast duckling with truffles
Caneton Braisé aux Navets: braised duckling with garlic & turnips
Caneton d'Albuféra: duckling with ham slices, butter, onions & wine
Caneton Farci à la Morvandelle: duckling with stuffing & ham
Caneton Grillé aux Pommes Reinettes: broiled duckling with potatoes in a cream sauce
Caneton "Ma Pomme": duckling with apples
Caneton Mulard au Citron: duckling with lemon
Caneton Nantais Poêlé aux Pêches: duckling with peaches
Caneton Rôti au Citron: roast duckling with lemon
Canette au Vinaigre de Xérès: young female duck in sherry vinegar
Canneberges: cranberries
Cantal: hard cheese
Capilotade de Volaille Paysanne: stew of chicken, carrots, turnips, onions, potatoes, celery, leeks & white wine
Câpres: capers
Caprice des Fins Gourmets: what a fussy gourmet would eat
Carafe: wine bottle
Carbonnade Flamande: braised beef & onions with beer
Cardinal: red cream fish sauce with puréed roe (fish eggs)
Cardons au Gratin: celery-like vegetable of the artichoke

Carpe

family with grated cheese & bread crumbs
Carême: chicken & veal with carrots, turnips, lettuce & asparagus tips
Carotte Vichy: sweet carrots
Carottes à la Crème: carrots in cream sauce
Carottes à la Flamande: carrots in butter with egg yolks & cream
Carottes à l'Aigre Doux: caramel carrots with vinegar sauce
Carottes à la Ménagère: carrots in broth, white wine & nutmeg
Carottes à la Paysanne: carrots in butter with bacon & onions
Carottes à l'Argenteuil: carrots in butter with white asparagus tips
Carottes à la Rhénanne: carrots in butter with onions & apples
Carottes au Beurre: carrots with butter
Carottes au Panais: carrots & parsnips in white stock
Carottes aux Cèpes: carrots in white wine & butter with mushrooms
Carottes aux Fines Herbes: glazed carrots with finely chopped herbs
Carottes aux Haricots Blancs: carrots with butter & navy beans
Carottes aux Oignons: carrots & onions in butter, cream sauce with egg yolks, milk & vinegar
Carottes Frites: carrots fried in bread crumbs
Carpe: Carp (fish)
Carpe à la Bière: sliced carp in butter with onions, celery & gingerbread in beer
Carpe à la Bourguignonne: carp in red wine with mushrooms & onions
Carpe à l'Alsacienne: carp with pike forcemeat in white wine, sauerkraut & potatoes
Carpe à la Mayonnaise: fried carp filets with mayonnaise & potatoes
Carpe à l'Ancienne: carp with bread crumbs, egg, cream & nutmeg in white wine
Carpe à la Polonaise: carp pieces in beer & red wine with onions, thyme, bay leaf, pepper corns, cloves, vinegar, sugar & almonds
Carpe à la Roumaine: carp with onions, lemon, tomatoes, garlic, white wine & sunflower oil
Carpe à l'Orientale: carp pieces in oil, white wine, shallots, almonds & saffron
Carpe au Bleu: carp in salted water with vinegar, butter,

Carpe

potatoes & horseradish sauce
Carpe au Choucroute: carp filets with sauerkraut in white wine sauce
Carpe au Paprika: carp pieces in white wine, butter, mushrooms & paprika sauce
Carpe aux Oignons: carp poached in white wine & onions
Carpe Bréteuil: broiled carp with butter, puff pastry with fish roe (eggs) & white wine sauce
Carpe Chambord: carp with bacon & truffles
Carpe en Matelote: carp pieces in red wine, brandy, mushrooms, onions & fried croutons
Carré d'Agneau Arlésienne: rack of lamb with tomatoes, eggplant & onions
Carré d'Agneau Aubergines au Gratin: rack of lamb, eggplant, grated cheese & bread crumbs
Carré d'Agneau aux Aromates: roast rack of lamb with spices
Carré d'Agneau aux Pommes Sarladaise: roast rack of lamb with potatoes & fried truffles
Carré d'Agneau Belle de Mai: rack of lamb or center rib chops
Carré d'Agneau de Pré Salé Sarladaise: rack of lamb with truffles & fried potatoes
Carré d'Agneau des Alpilles aux Petits Tomates Farcis Niçois: rack of Alpine lamb, tomatoes, hard boiled eggs & vegetables
Carré d'Agneau Persillé: rack of lamb roasted pink with parsley
Carré d'Agneau Pré Salé: rack of lamb naturally salty
Carré d'Agneau Provençale: roast rack of lamb with garlic sauce
Carré d'Agneau Rôti: roast rack of lamb
Carré d'Agneau Rôti Aux Herbes: roast rack of lamb with herbs
Carré d'Agneau Rôti aux Herbes de Provence: roast rack of lamb with garlic & herbs
Carré d'Agnelet aux Herbes de Provence: rack of young spring lamb roasted with herbs
Carré de Boeuf au Maïs: larded ribs of beef with pork & garlic with corn
Carré de l'Est: soft mild flavored cheese
Carré de Porc: rib roast of pork
Carré de Porc à la Paysanne: roasted pork loin with onions & potatoes

Cassoulet

Carré de Porc à la Soissonaise: roast pork loin with navy beans
Carré de Porc au Choucroute: roast pork loin with sauerkraut, potatoes & gravy
Carré de Porc au Chou Rouge: roast pork loin with red cabbage & gravy
Carré de Porc aux Choux de Bruxelles: pork loin with Brussels sprouts
Carré de Porc aux Purées Diverses: roast pork loin with purée of lentils, celery, onions, peas or potatoes
Carré de Porc Fumé: smoked pork loin, sauerkraut, red cabbage or spinach & boiled or mashed potatoes
Carré de Porc Rôti: roast loin of pork
Carré de Veau: rib roast of veal
Carrelet: flounder
Carrelet aux Oignons: flounder with onions
Cassata au Marasquin: Italian ice cream with diced fruit, macaroons & cherry liqueur
Cassate: ice cream cake with candied fruit
Casse-Croûte: long sandwich on French bread
Casse Museau Landais: hard French cake of eggs, cheese, olive oil & brandy
Cassemuseaux François Ier: dessert cheese, brandy & egg cake
Casserolette d'Escargots au Champagne et Noisettes: small casserole of snails with champagne & hazelnuts
Casserolette de Filets de Sole: casserole of filet of sole
Cassolette de Brochet Homardine: pike with lobster sauce
Cassolette d'Ecrevisses Marinière: crayfish (lobster) with tomato, cheese, garlic & artichoke heart sauce
Cassolette d'Escargots à l'Anis: baked licorice flavored snails
Cassolette d'Escargots aux Noix: baked snails & nuts
Cassolette de Filets de Sole: baked filets of sole
Cassolette de Fruits de Mer: dish of various seafoods in a sauce
Cassolette de Moules au Citron: mussels with lemon
Cassolette de Queues d'Ecrevisses: small casserole of crayfish tails
Cassolette de Sole Crocodile: sole cooked in a small flame proof dish
Cassoulet: dish with white beans, goose, pork, mutton, duck, sausage, onions, garlic & tomatoes with bread crumbs
Cassoulet au Confit d'Oie: casserole of white beans & goose

Cassoulet

Cassoulet au Confit Landais: white bean & goose casserole
Cassoulet de Castelnaudary: baked beans with pork rinds, pork, salted goose & sausage
Cassoulet de Toulouse: baked beans with pork rinds, pork, preserved goose & sausage
Caviar: salted roe (fish eggs)
Caviar à Pandalouse: boiled onion with caviar mixture of egg, bread crumbs, butter & pepper
Caviar de Béluga: Persian caviar
Caviar Frais d'Iran: fresh Persian caviar
Caviar Malossol: Persian Malossol caviar
Caviar Namur: salmon caviar
Caviar Niçoise: caviar with capers, black olives & brandy
Caviar Pressé: caviar with French dressing & chopped onions
Cayettes: sausage
Céleri: Celery
Céleri à la Bonne Femme: celery with potatoes & mayonnaise
Céleri à la Génevoise: celery with cream sauce, bread crumbs & grated cheese
Céleri a la Hongroise: celery with onion & aniseed with paprika sauce
Céleri a la Moëlle: celery covered with ox marrow in brown sauce
Céleri à la Sauce au Malaga: celery in wine sauce
Céleri à la Sauce Hollandaise: celery in white stock & Hollandaise sauce (egg yolk, butter & lemon juice)
Céleri à la Tessinoise: celery batter fried with sugar
Céleri à l'Espagnole: celery in brown sauce with shallots, garlic & tomatoes
Céleri à l'Italienne: celery with Parmesan cheese in butter or tomato sauce
Céleri au Jus: celery in bacon fat with onions, carrots & veal gravy
Céleri au Sauce Madère: celery in wine sauce
Céleri Braisé: celery on top of onions, carrots & bacon fat in wine sauce
Céleri Farci au Roquefort: celery stuffed with Roquefort cheese
Céleri en Branches: celery in butter with bacon, onions & carrots
Céleri Milanaise: celery with butter & Parmesan cheese with a fried egg

Cerf

Céleri Rapé Remoulade: shredded celery in mustard sauce
Céleri-Rave: celery root (celeriac)
Céleri-Rave à la Grecque: celery root with apples, tomatoes & onions in white wine
Céleri-Rave à la Hollandaise: celery root in lemon juice with Hollandaise sauce (egg yolks & butter)
Céleri-Rave à la Méranienne: baked celery root with bacon, white stock, butter & sour cream
Céleri-Rave au Jus: celery root in veal gravy
Céleri-Rave au Parmesan: celery root baked with bread crumbs & grated cheese
Céleri-Rave Braisé: celery root in wine sauce
Céleri-Rave Frit à l-Italienne: deep fried celery root with tomato sauce
Céleri-Rave Marine: celery root in oil & vinegar with mustard
Célestines de Fruits de Mer: seafood in a broth
Cendré de la Brie: cow's milk cheese
Centre de Baudroie à l'Américaine: anglerfish in brandy, tomatoes & white wine
Cèpes: wild, flat mushrooms
Cèpes à la Bordelaise: sautéed large mushrooms & garlic
Cèpes à la Crème: mushrooms & onions in butter cream sauce
Cèpes à la Moldavienne: mushrooms sautéed with shallots in sour cream with chives & fennel (licorice flavored herb)
Cèpes à la Nordique: sautéed mushrooms in sour cream
Cèpes à la Piémontaise: mushrooms caps with stems & garlic
Cèpes à l'Arléquin: sautéed mushrooms, onions, carrots & celery root, white wine & tomato sauce
Cèpes à la Russe: buttered mushrooms & onions in sour cream with fennel (licorice flavored herb)
Cèpes à la Toulousaine: sautéed mushrooms, onions, shallots, garlic, tomatoes & ham
Cèpes Farcis: mushrooms caps with stems, onions, tomato sauce & bread crumbs
Cèpes Frites: fried mushrooms caps
Cèpes Grilleés: marinated mushrooms in butter & grilled
Cèpes Provençale: mushrooms sautéed with garlic
Cèpes Sautées: sautéed mushrooms
Céréales: cereals
Cerf: red deer
Cerf Berny: roast marinated deer with tarts, lentil purée & potatoes

Cerf

Cerf à l'Allemande: roast marinated deer with grated rye bread, red wine, cinnamon & brown sugar
Cerf à la Polonaise: marinated deer in white stock, sour cream, sauerkraut & fennel (licorice flavored herb)
Cerises: cherries
Cerises au Vin Rouge: cherries in red wine with sugar, cinnamon, red currant jelly & lady fingers
Cerises Eldorado: cherries in vanilla syrup & brandy
Cerises Frascati: cherries in Kirsch liqueur with whipped cream
Cerises Giboulées: cherries over ice cream
Cerises Henry IV: puff pastry tarts with red currant jelly, almond cream, Kirsch flavored cherries & meringues
Cerises Valéria: tarts filled with red currant cream, cherries, red wine & meringue
Cerises Van Dyck: cherries in white wine with sugar on vanilla cream
Cervelas de Fruits de Mer: sausage of seafood
Cervelas Rémoulade: sliced hot dog in mustard-mayonnaise sauce
Cervelas Vinaigrette: sliced hot dog in oil & vinegar sauce & onions
Cervelles: brains
Cervelles au Beurre Noir: brains in brown butter
Cervelles de Veau aux Câpres: veal brains with capers
Cetéaux: small sole (fish)
Chabichou: soft goat's milk cheese
Chabot: chub (fish)
Chabrillan: tomato soup with garnish
Chabris: goat's milk cheese
Chambéry: salad of lobster, salmon, tomato, artichoke bottoms, gherkins & lettuce with mayonnaise & vinegar
Champenois: cheese from cow's milk
Champignons: mushrooms
Champignons à la Bordelaise: mushrooms in red wine & brown sauce
Champignons à la Capucine: sautéed mushrooms with garlic & pigeon
Champignons à la Crème: sautéed mushrooms in cream
Champignons à la Grecque: marinated mushrooms
Champignons à la Provençale: mushrooms with garlic & tomatoes
Champignons au Beurre: mushrooms with butter
Champignons au Porto: mushrooms in butter with wine

Charlotte

Champignons de Paris: common mushrooms
Champignons de Paris Bordelaise: sautéed mushrooms with garlic & olive oil
Champignons Frais au Beurre: fresh mushrooms in butter
Champignons Farcis Périgourdine: stuffed mushrooms with truffles & goose liver
Champignons Grillés Bouguignonne: grilled mushrooms in red wine
Champignons Sautés: sautéed mushrooms
Champigny: puff pastry with apricot jam & pieces with Kirsch
Changement de Garniture: alternative garnish
Chanterelle: small yellow mushroom
Chantilly: whipped cream added to Hollandaise sauce (butter & lemoned egg yolks) or whipped cream
Chaource: cow's milk cheese
Chapon: fish or young fattened chicken or bread crusts with garlic & olive oil
Chapon à la Bressane: capon (chicken) sautéed with mushrooms, white wine, cream & egg yolks
Chapon à la Provencale: pinkish-red fish, tomato sauce, garlic & oil
Chapon à l'Estragon: roast capon (chicken) with tarragon
Chapon Farci: stuffed pinkish-red fish
Chapon Farci aux Scampis: pinkish-red fish with scampis (shrimp)
Charbonnée: pork stew thickened with pork blood
Charbonnée Comme Autrefois: old fashioned pork stew
Charbonnée de Lile: pork with bacon & onion in wine sauce
Charbonnier: coalfish
Charcuterie: delicatessen or cold cuts
Charcuterie Maison: assortment of cooked meats in the style of the restaurant
Chardonnade de Crustacés: assorted shellfish
Charlotte: custard gelatin mold with sponge cakes or macaroons or mold lined with lady fingers or sponge cake with Bavarian cream & fruit
Charlotte aux Noisettes et Miel: sponge cake slices with creamy hazelnuts & honey
Charlotte aux Noisettes Pralinées: sponge cake with praline flavor
Charlotte Chantilly: dish with Bavarian cream & whipped cream, small meringues & praline powder
Charlotte de Fruits: fruit mixture with slices of buttered bread & sugar

Charlotte

Charlotte de Pommes: buttered peach slices filled with apple purée
Charlotte Duc du Praslin: dish with sponge cake with whipped creams or mousses
Charlotte Malakoff: lady fingers with almond powder & Kirsch blended with whipped cream
Charlotte Plombière: lady fingers with a very rich cream
Charlotte Russe: lady fingers with whipped cream
Charollais à la Bourguignonne: braised beef with red wine, mushrooms, small onions & strips of fat
Charollais en Croûte: filet of beef in puff pastry baked with a cream sauce
Charollais Vigneronne: beef prepared in vine leaves
Charolles: goat's milk cheese
Chartreuse de Perdreaux Alsacienne: partridges & cabbage in a casserole
Chartreuse Villeneuvoise: partridge with cabbage & vegetables
Chasse Royale: cooked game arranged in a pyramid
Chasseur, Sauce: sauce of white wine, Madeira wine, mushrooms, shallots & tomato sauce
Châtaignes: chestnuts
Châteaubriand: tender steak from the filet of beef or wine
Châteaubriand aux Pommes: filet steak with french fried potatoes
Châteaubriand Béarnaise: beef tenderloin with Béarnaise sauce (white wine, shallots, egg yolks & herbs)
Châteaubriand Bouquetière Flambé Pour Deux: filet of beef served flaming with vegetables for 2 people
Châteaubriand en Brioche: filet of beef in a pastry shell
Châteaubriand en Croûte: beef tenderloin in a pastry crust
Châteaubriand Garni: grilled filet of beef
Châteaubriand Grillé: broiled filet of beef
Châteaubriand Sauce Béarnaise: grilled filet of beef with red wine, shallots, egg yolks & herb sauce
Châteaubriand Sauce Choron: filet of beef with a tomato red wine sauce
Château: salad of frog's legs, lettuce & watercress with oil & vinegar dressing or mayonnaise
Chaud Froid de Volaille: poached chicken with hot sauce in aspic
Chaud Froid: cream sauce for game, fish, chicken or meat served cold
Chausson: puff pastry of fruit, chocolate, etc.

Chou-Fleur

Chausson de Crabe Baie St. Jean: puff pastry with crabmeat
Chausson de Homard à l'Américaine: puff pastry with lobster chunks in a cream wine sauce
Chausson de Morilles: mushroom puff pastry
Chausson de Moules: turnover with mussels
Chèvre: goat cheese
Chevreau au Champagne: kid goat in champagne
Chevreuil: deer (venison)
Chevreuil Rôti, Sauce Groseille: roast venison in currant sauce
Chicorée: type of endive
Chiffonade: salad dressing of vinaigrette with hard boiled eggs & beetroot
Chinois: Chinese oranges (Mandarin oranges)
Chipirons: squid
Chipolatas: sausage similar to a chorizo (Mexican)
Chivry: cream sauce for poultry, eggs or fish
Choclatine: chocolate cake with chocolate butter cream
Chocolat Truffé: very creamy chocolate (bars)
Chops d'Agneau à l'Anglaise Sauce Menthe: grilled lamb chops with mint sauce
Choron: sauce for tournedos, lamb nuggets of artichoke hearts, green peas & potatoes
Chou: cabbage or pastry similar to cream puffs
Choucroute: sauerkraut
Choucroute Alsacienne: sauerkraut with salt pork, ham & sausages
Choucroute Riche: sauerkraut in white wine with ham, bacon or pickled goose, frankfurters, sausages & boiled potatoes
Chou Farci: stuffed cabbage
Chou Farci a là Nantaise: cabbage leaves filled with salt pork, onions, shallots & crumbs
Chou-Fleur: cauliflower
Chou-Fleur a la Cardinale: boiled cauliflower with Parmesan cheese & white sauce with Cayenne pepper
Chou-Fleur a la Florentine: cauliflower with spinach, butter, creamy cheese sauce & Parmesan cheese
Chou-Fleur a la Francaise: cauliflower with nutmeg & butter sauce
Chou-Fleur au Beurre: cauliflower in butter
Chou-Fleur au Gratin: cauliflower with grated cheese & bread crumbs
Chou-Fleur aux Queues d'Ecrevisses: cauliflower with crayfish tails (lobster) & crayfish sauce

Chou-Fleur

Chou-Fleur Frite: fried cauliflower
Chou-Fleur Sautée: sautéed cauliflower
Chou-Fleur Sauce Hollandaise: cauliflower with Hollandaise sauce
Chou-Fleur Vinaigrette: cauliflower with oil & vinegar dressing
Choux à la Crème: cream puffs
Choux de Bruxelles: Brussels sprouts
Choux de Bruxelles à la Crème: Brussels sprouts with cream sauce
Choux de Bruxelles à la Grandmère: Brussels sprouts sautéed with onions, bacon & croutons
Choux de Bruxelles à l'Italienne: Brussels sprouts with Parmesan cheese, butter & anchovy filets
Ciboulettes: chives
Cîteaux: cow's milk cheese
Citron: lemon
Citron Vert: lime
Civet: red wine stew
Civet d'Abatis d'Oie à la Picarde: goose giblets stewed with red wine & brown sauce
Civet de Canard au Bourgueil: duck stewed in a pot
Civet de Caneton aux Châtaignes: duckling stew with wine & chestnuts
Civet de Chevreuil: marinated diced venison with red wine
Civet de Coq et de Pieds de Porc au Vin de Cahors: rooster stew with pig's feet in wine
Civet de Langouste Crème: creamed lobster tails in a stew
Civet de Lièvre: rabbit stew in brandy, onions & red wine
Civet de Lièvre à la Bruxelloise: rabbit stew with bacon, onions & grapes
Civet de Lièvre à la Flamande: rabbit stew with red wine, onions, brown sugar, & croutons with red currant jam
Civet de Lièvre à l'Allemande: rabbit stew with wine, vinegar, onions, mushrooms & bacon
Civet de Lièvre à la Lorraine: rabbit stew with red wine
Civet de Lièvre à l'Ancienne: rabbit stew with shallots, garlic, bacon, red wine, tomatoes & mushrooms
Civet de Lièvre à la Solognote: wild hare stew with wine, herbs & mushrooms
Civet de Lièvre au Corton: rabbit stew in white wine
Civet de Porcelet: piglet stew
Civet de Porcelet Provençale: piglet stew with tomatoes, mushrooms, eggplant, garlic & shallots
Civet de Poularde de Bresse aux Vieux Beaune: chicken

Coeurs

stew in red wine
Civet de Ris de Veau: veal sweetbread stew
Clafoutis: custard pie with fruit or thick pastry with fruit
Clamart, à la: served with green peas
Clams: like steamers
Clémentine: kumquats
Cochon: pig
Cochon de Lait: suckling pig
Cochon de Lait à la Bavaroise: suckling pig roasted, veal gravy & cole slaw with bacon bits
Cochon de Lait à l'Allemande: roast suckling pig with apple slices & currants
Cochon de Lait à l'Arlésienne: suckling pig with sausage & sauerkraut
Cochon de Lait à l'Américaine: roast suckling pig with sausage, onions, bread crumbs & eggs
Cochon de Lait à l'Anglaise: roast suckling pig with sage, onions, apples & currants
Cochon de Lait à la Piémontaise: roast suckling pig with rice, truffles & tomato sauce
Cochon de Lait à la Poloanise: roast suckling pig with cabbage & ham
Cochon de Lait à la Russe: roast unseasoned suckling pig with sour cream
Cochon de Lait à l'Italienne: suckling pig with rice, salami & cheese
Cochon de Lait aux Pruneaux: roast suckling pig with prunes
Cochon de Lait en Gelée: suckling pig in aspic
Cochon de Lait Farci de Foie de Porc: roast suckling pig stuffed with chopped pork liver, nutmeg & bread crumbs
Cochon de Lait Persillée: roast suckling pig with onions & garlic
Cocktail de Crevettes: shrimp cocktail
Cocktail de Crevettes Fine Champagne: shrimp cocktail in cognac
Cocktail de Fruits de Mer: seafood cocktail
Cocktail de Homard Moscovite: Russian lobster cocktail
Cocktail de Pamplemousse: grapefruit cocktail
Coeur de Boeuf: beef heart
Coeur de Filet Grillé: broiled beef tenderloin
Coeur de Laitue aux Queues d'Ecrevisses: heart of lettuce with lobster tails
Coeur de Veau: veal heart
Coeurs d'Artichauts Vinaigrette: artichoke hearts with vinai-

Coeurs

grette sauce
Coeurs de Palmiers: hearts of palm with vinaigrette sauce
Coeurs de Palmiers au Jambon: heart of palm with ham
Coing: quince (berry)
Colin: hake (fish)
Colin à la Meunière: hake filet in butter & lemon
Colin à l'Ancienne: boiled hake with caper sauce & gherkins
Colin à la Polonaise: hake filets fried with hard boiled eggs
Colin à la Toulousaine: hake poached in bouillon with white wine sauce, mushrooms, onions, olives & pike dumplings
Colin à l'Oseille: hake braised in white wine & butter with onions, bacon & sorrel (lettuce like herb)
Colin au Vin Rouge: hake in red wine & shallots
Colin Gambetta: poached hake filets with green herb sauce & truffles
Colin Léopold: hake & scallops in white wine with lobster sauce & truffles
Colombine: croquette with semolina (wheat) & Parmesan cheese
Compote: fruit with wine or fruit sauces
Compote d'Abricots: apricots in vanilla syrup with almonds & Kirsch liqueur
Compote d'Ananas: pineapple in vanilla syrup & Kirsch liqueur
Compote de Bananes: bananas in vanilla syrup with Kirsch liqueur or rum
Compote de Cerises: cherries in vanilla syrup & Kirsch liqueur
Compote de Figues: figs in vanilla syrup & Kirsch liqueur
Compote de Fraises: strawberries in vanilla syrup
Compote de Framboises: raspberries in vanilla syrup
Compote de Pêches: peaches in vanilla syrup & Kirsch
Compote de Poires: pears in vanilla syrup & lemon juice
Compote de Pommes: apples in lemon juice & white wine OR apple sauce
Compote de Rhubarbe: rhubarb in vanilla syrup
Compote Frâiche: fresh fruit in vanilla syrup
Compotes Assorties: assorted poached fruit
Comté: hard cheese
Concombre: cucumber
Concombre à la Crème: cucumbers in cream sauce
Concombre à la Duchesse: cucumbers with chicken forcemeat, sour cream & grated cheese
Concombre à l'Allemande: cucumber sautéed with onions,

Consommé

bacon, vinegar & brown sauce
Concombre à l'Andalouse: cucumber in tomato sauce with Parmesan cheese
Concombre à la Romaine: sautéed cucumber with Roman sauce (caramelized sugar, vinegar, pine nuts, black currants & brown sauce)
Concombre à la Saxonne: cucumber in butter with onions & sour cream
Concombre à la Tsarine: cucumber with fennel (licorice herb)
Concombre à l'Italienne: cucumber with bread crumbs, egg yolks, grated cheese & hard boiled eggs
Concombre Clermont: cucumber in butter with artichoke bottoms
Concombre Farci: stuffed cucumber
Concombre Frit: fried cucumber
Concombre Glacé: glazed cucumbers
Concombres Salade: cucumber salad
Concombre Stéphanie: cucumber with pork sausage, truffles, goose liver pâté & pork with crayfish (lobster) butter
Congre: conger eel (fish)
Congre à la Brochette: skewered conger eel with tartar sauce
Congre à l'Espagnole: stewed conger eel, red wine, vinegar, onions, red peppers, garlic & thyme
Confit: various foods in its own fat or vegetables or fruits preserved in sugar, vinegar & brandy
Confit de Canard: duck cooked in its own fat
Confit de Canard au Poivre Vert: duck in its own fat with green peppers
Confit de Canard aux Cèpes: duck in its own fat with mushrooms
Confit de Pigeon au Foie Gras et Truffé: pigeon stewed in its own fat with livers & truffles
Confit de Porc: pork cooked in its own fat
Confit d'Oie: goose cooked in its own fat
Confit d'Oie aux Pommes: goose in its own fat with potatoes or apples
Confit d'Oie aux Haricots Blancs: goose in its own fat with white beans
Confit d'Oie des Landes: goose cooked in its own fat
Confiture de Marrons: sugared purée of chestnuts
Consommé: clear broth
Consommé Soup: meat or poultry broth with vegetables

Consommé

strained of all fat
Consommé à la Reine: thickened chicken broth with sliced chicken
Consommé à l'Essence de Piments: cold broth with slices of pepper or pimento
Consommé à l'Oeuf: clear egg broth
Consommé Andalouse: beef broth with tomatoes, chopped beef, peppers & vegetables
Consommé aux Ailerons Farcis: chicken broth with chicken wings
Consommé aux Pâtes: soup broth with noodles
Consommé aux Profiterolles: broth with puff pastries
Consommé Belle Hélène: strong chicken broth with crepes
Consommé Célestine: chicken broth with pancakes with chicken & herbs
Consommé Chasseur: game broth with mushrooms, port wine with pastry stuffed with mousse of pheasant
Consommé Chasseur aux Profiterolles: game broth with tapioca, mushrooms and round pastries
Consommé Chaud: hot broth
Consommé Chaud ou Froid: hot or cold broth
Consommé Clair: clear meat broth
Consommé Colbert: vegetable soup with port wine
Consommé d'Ecrevisses: crayfish (lobster) broth
Consommé de Volaille: chicken broth
Consommé en Gelée: jellied broth
Consommé Froid: cold broth
Consommé Gelée: jellied broth
Consommé Julienne: clear broth with sliced vegetables
Consommé Madrilène: broth with tomato concentrate
Consommé Moëlle au Cerfeuil: bone marrow broth with chervil (like parsley)
Consommé Queue de Boeuf: broth of oxtail, carrots & turnips
Consommé St. Hubert: strong broth, wine & pieces of custard
Consommé Vermicelle: broth with noodles & grated cheese
Contre Filet: sirloin steak
Contre Filet au Gratin Dauphinois: sirloin steak with potatoes & cheese
Conversation: pastry tart
Copeaux: small cakes (petits fours)
Coprin Chevelu: mushroom
Coq: rooster

Coquilles

Coq à la Morvandelle: rooster
Coq au Chambertin: rooster in red wine
Coq au Jambon Nivernaise: braised rooster with diced ham, mushrooms & brandy
Coq au Morilles: rooster with mushrooms
Coq au Reisling: rooster in Reisling wine
Coq au Vin: rooster in red wine
Coq au Vinaigre: rooster cooked in vinegar
Coq au Vin à la Champenoise: rooster with pork, mushrooms, onions in red wine
Coq au Vin d'Arbois: rooster cooked in wine
Coq au Vin de Bourgueil: rooster cooked in red wine
Coq au Vin de Champigny: rooster in wine sauce
Coq au Vin de Charturgue: rooster with pork, onions & red wine
Coq au Vin Jaune: rooster in wine sauce
Coq au Vin Jaune et Morilles: rooster in yellow wine sauce with mushrooms
Coq au Vin Provençale: rooster with onions, pork, butter, garlic, brandy & red wine
Coq au Vin Rouge de Champagne: rooster with red wine
Coq au Vin Vigneronne: rooster in wine sauce
Coq en Pâté: rooster in pastry with glaze
Coq Sauté aux Vins des Graves: Sautéed rooster with wine
Coquelet: young rooster
Coquelet à la Crème: rooster with cream sauce
Coquelet à l'Ail: rooster with garlic
Coquelet à la Moutarde: rooster with mustard
Coquelet au Vin d'Auvergne: rooster in wine
Coquelet aux Ecrevisses: rooster with lobster
Coques: cake with jam or chocolate
Coquillages: various shellfish
Coquilles: scallop shells
Coquilles St. Jacques: creamed scallops in a shell
Coquilles St. Jacques à la Provençale: creamed scallops with garlic sauce
Coquilles St. Jacques Champagne: scallops in champagne
Coquilles St. Jacques a Cidre: creamed scallops with cider
Coquilles St. Jacques au Naturel: plain scallops
Coquilles St. Jacques au Wiskey: creamed scallops with whiskey
Coquilles St. Jacques Bercy: scallops with Bercy sauce (white wine, shallots & fish broth)
Coquilles St. Jacques Beurre Blanc: scallops with butter &

Coquilles

shallots in wine & wine vinegar
Coquilles St. Jacques Bourguignonne: scallops with red wine & mushrooms
Coquilles St. Jacques Brétagne: scallops & mushrooms with sauce & cheese on top
Coquilles St. Jacques en Brochette: scallops on skewer
Coquilles St. Jacques en Brochette Forestière: skewered scallops & mushrooms
Coquilles St. Jacques Nantaise: scallops in shell with crawfish tail sauce of butter, cream & sometimes cheese
Coquilles St. Jacques Provençale: scallops in garlic butter
Corbeille des Fruits: basket or tray of fresh fruit
Cornet au Jambon à la Russe: sliced ham stuffed with truffled goose liver on vegetables with hard boiled eggs & gelatin
Cornichons: dill pickles
Côte à l'Ardennaise: pork chops or cutlets with juniper berries with onions & potatoes
Côte d'Agneau: lamb chop
Côte d'Agneau St. Hubert: lamb chops with game sauce or soup of lentils, sherry, mushrooms & tapioca
Côte d'Agneau sur Gril: broiled lamb chops
Côte de Boeuf: rib of beef
Côte de Boeuf à la Moëlle: rib steak with marrow
Côte de Boeuf Grillée: broiled rib of beef
Côte de Boeuf Grillée au Feu de Bois: rib roast grilled over wood fire
Côte de Boeuf Marchand de Vin: rib of beef with onion, butter, mushroom, marrow & red wine sauce
Côte de Boeuf Poêlée: rib roast of beef in casserole
Côte de Charollais à l'Estragon: rib roast with tarragon
Côte de Porc: pork chop
Côte de Porc à l'Auvergnate: braised pork chops with cabbage, cream & white wine
Côte de Porc Frites: pork chops with french fries
Côte de Porc Grillée Maître d'Hotel: grilled pork chops
Côte de Veau: veal chops
Côte de Veau Casserole: Veal chop casserole
Côte de Veau Sauce Madère: veal chops with sherry sauce
Côtellette de Brochet: steaks or slices of pike
Côtellette de Volaille à la Kiev: chicken breast fried in butter (chicken Kiev)
Côtelette d'Agneau: Lamb cutlet
Côtelette d'Agneau Grillée: grilled lamb cutlet
Côtelette de Chevreuil a la Solognote: venison cutlets on

Coupe

toast
Côtelettes de Poisson: fish cutlets
Côtelettes de Porc Piquante: pork cutlets with onions in hot sauce
Côtelettes Korniloff: chicken cutlets with cream
Côtelettes de Veau au Petit Lard: veal cutlets with bacon, onion & white wine
Côtelettes de Veau Morvandelle: veal cutlets with ham & onions in brown sauce with potatoes & mushrooms
Côtelettes de Volaille: chicken cutlets
Côtes d'Agneau: lamb chops
Côtes d'Agneau Haricots Verts: rack of lamb with green beans
Côtes de Porc: pork chops
Côtes de Veau: veal chops
Côtes de Veau à l'Angevine: veal chops with white wine sauce
Côtes de Veau aux Epinards: veal chops on spinach
Côtes de Veau aux Morilles: veal chops with mushrooms, cream & butter sauce
Côtes de Veau Clamart: veal chops with little peas
Côtes de Veau Panées et Sautées Beurre: veal cutlet breaded & sautéed in butter
Cotriade: fish stew with potatoes
Cou: neck
Cou d'Oie à l'Oseille: goose neck with sorrel (lettuce like herb)
Cou d'Oie Farci: stuffed goose neck with truffles in white wine
Couennes de Porc: pork rind
Coulis: puréed fish, shellfish & vegetable sauce
Coulommiers: cheese similar to brie
Coupe: sundae
Coupe Adélina: chocolate ice cream on strawberries in Kirsch liqueur with whipped cream
Coupe a la Brésilienne: pineapple with Maraschino liqueur & lemon ice
Coupe à la Napolitaine: lemon ice with fruit mixture in liqueur with apricot jelly & whipped cream
Coupe à l'Andalouse: orange pieces in Maraschino liqueur & with lemon ice & whipped cream
Coupe à la Niçoise: fruit mixture with Curaçao liqueur, orange ice, peaches in Maraschino liqueur, whipped cream & glazed cherries

Coupe

Coupe à l'Arlésienne: vanilla ice cream with fruit in Kirsch liqueur with pear in vanilla syrup & apricot sauce
Coupe à la Royale: vanilla ice cream with strawberries in Kirsch liqueur with whipped cream
Coupe a la Suédoise: vanilla ice cream with apple purée, apples, red currant jelly & whipped cream
Coupe à la Tsarine: lemon ice with cherries & whipped cream
Coupe Alexandra: fruit mixture in Kirsch liqueur with strawberry ice & strawberries
Coupe Américaine: pineapple ice with pineapple pieces & macaroons, whipped cream, caramelized violets & strawberries in Kirsch
Coupe Barbarina: strawberry ice cream with macaroons in Maraschino syrup with chocolate cream, whipped cream & pineapple pieces
Coupe Bébé: pineapple & raspberry ice with strawberries, whipped cream & caramelized violets
Coupe Carrousel: vanilla, coffee & strawberry ice cream with fruit & whipped cream
Coupe Claire Dux: fruit mixture in Kirsch & hazelnut ice cream, whipped cream & strawberries
Coupe Clo-Clo: glazed chestnuts in Maraschino liqueur with vanilla ice cream, whipped cream & strawberry purée
Coupe Créole: pineapple & bananas in Kirsch liqueur with lemon ice with rum & whipped cream
Coupe Dame Blanche: almond ice cream with peach, white currant jelly & lemon ice
Coupe de Fruits à la Fine: bowl of fresh fruit in cognac
Coupe de Fruits Frais: fresh fruit cup
Coupe de Glace — Crème Fine: sundae with various sauces
Coupe Denise: coffee ice cream with liqueured nuts & whipped cream
Coupe Diable Rouge: strawberry ice with cherries in red wine & raspberry syrup, whipped cream & strawberry purée
Coupe Divine: peach in Cointreau liqueur with chocolate ice cream, heavy cream, meringues, caramelized violets & whipped cream
Coupe Edna May: vanilla ice cream with cherry compote, whipped cream & raspberry purée
Coupe Elisabeth: poached cherries in Kirsch liqueur & cherry brandy with whipped cream & cinnamon
Coupe Emma Clavé: vanilla ice cream with cherries in Kirsch liqueur & raspberry purée

Coupe

Coupe Eugenie: vanilla ice cream with glazed chestnuts in Maraschino liqueur, whipped cream & caramelized violets

Coupe Francois Joseph: pineapple in Kirsch liqueur with orange ice & whipped cream

Coupe Frou-Frou: vanilla ice cream with peach, whipped cream & glazed cherries

Coupe Glacée aux Fraises: strawberry sundae

Coupe Glace Vanille au Gingombre: vanilla ice cream with ginger

Coupe Hélène: vanilla ice cream with pears in Kirsch liqueur, chocolate sauce & caramelized violets

Coupe Iris: cherries in red wine with sugar & cinnamon with strawberry mousse, whipped cream & chocolate bits

Coupe Jacqueline: fresh fruit in liqueur with lemon & strawberry ice cream, almonds & glazed cherries

Coupe Jacques: fruits in liqueur with lemon & strawberry ice cream or half orange & half strawberry parfait with Maraschino cherries, whipped cream & brandied pineapple

Coupe Jubilé: cherries in Kirsch liqueur with vanilla ice cream, whipped cream & pistachios

Coupe Louis: peach ice cream and apricot with marzipan cake, whipped cream & strawberry purée

Coupe Louis XV: strawberry mousse with gold plums, peach jam & whipped cream

Coupe Maharadja: apricot ice with almonds, pears in liqueur, red currant jelly, whipped cream & ginger biscuits

Coupe Malmaison: vanilla ice cream with grapes, whipped cream & spun sugar

Coupe Médicis: raspberry mousse with strawberries & raspberries in Maraschino liqueur & whipped cream

Coupe Metternich: pineapple pieces with raspberry ice & vanilla whipped cream

Coupe Méxicaine: tangerine ice with pineapple pieces

Coupe Mireille: vanilla & red currant ice cream with nectarines, white currants, whipped cream & spun sugar

Coupe Mozart: vanilla & almond ice cream with peaches, raspberry syrup, whipped cream & almonds

Coupe Olivier: fresh fruit ice cream sundae

Coupe Petit Duc: vanilla ice cream with peach, red currant jelly & lemon ice

Coupe Piémont: nut ice cream, chocolate sauce & whipped cream

Coupe Portugaise: pineapple in Maraschino liqueur with orange ice, whipped cream & sour cherries

Coupe

Coupe Sahara: vanilla ice cream with peach in Kirsch liqueur with raspberry ice, whipped cream, pineapple & glazed cherries

Coupe Santa Lucia: vanilla ice cream with grapes in sugar & liqueur, chocolate sauce, macaroons, whipped cream & raspberry sauce

Coupes Assorties: assorted sundaes

Coupe Savoy: fruit mixture in Anisetté (licorice flavored liqueur) with coffee & violet ice

Coupe Singapore: lemon ice with pineapple slices in Arrak liqueur with macaroons

Coupe St. Martin: fruit mixture with Maraschino liqueur, lemon & raspberry ices, whipped cream & strawberries

Coupe Sublime: vanilla ice cream with whipped cream, grated pumpernickel & cocoa

Coupe Sylvia: bananas in orange juice & Kirsch liqueur with hazelnut ice cream & whipped cream

Coupe Tous Parfums: all flavors of sundaes

Coupe Tutti Frutti: strawberry, lemon & pineapple ices with fruit in Kirsch liqueur

Coupe Vénus: vanilla ice cream with peach & strawberries with whipped cream

Coupe Véra Schwarz: fruit in Maraschino liqueur with raspberry ice, whipped cream & pistachios

Coupe Victoria: fruit mixture in cognac with strawberry & pistachio ices

Coupe Walewska: vanilla ice cream with peaches in Kirsch liqueur, whipped cream & strawberries

Courgette: squash

Courgettes Farcies: stuffed zucchini squash

Couscous: broth with chick peas, assorted vegetables & spicy sauce with chicken, ham or sausage over semolina (wheat grain)

Crabe: hard shelled crab

Crabe à la Bordelaise: crab with mushrooms & Bordeaux wine sauce on toast or croutons

Crabe à la Diable: crab in butter with onions, Cayenne pepper, cream sauce, mustard powder, Worcestershire sauce, chili sauce & bread crumbs

Crabe à la Grecque: crab with onions, leeks, butter, tomatoes, garlic, mussels, herbs & saffron rice

Crabe à la Méxicaine: crab with onions, green peppers, garlic, mustard powder, Worcestershire sauce & cheese sauce

Crabe à la Portugaise: crab with onions, mushrooms,

Crème

tomatoes & parsley
Crabe à l'Indienne: crab with curry sauce
Crabe à l'Italienne: crab with onions, parsley, garlic, tomato sauce & Parmesan cheese
Crabe Baltimore: crab with butter, shallots, Worcestershire sauce, Cayenne pepper, mustard powder & Mornay sauce (creamy cheese sauce)
Crabe Farcie: deviled crab
Crabe Maryland: crab in cream with Cayenne pepper & cognac on toast or croutons
Crabe Nelson: crab with cream sauce, oysters & grated Parmesan cheese
Crabe Valencia: crab with onions, mushrooms, red & green peppers, garlic, mustard powder, Worcestershire sauce, Cayenne pepper, Parmesan cheese & Mornay sauce (creamy cheese sauce)
Crécy: puréed carrot & rice soup
Crème: cream OR creamed soups
Crème à la Française: soup with curried chicken with cream & rice
Crème à la Rhubarbe: rhubarb purée & cream
Crème Américane: vanilla egg cream custard with sugar
Crème Argenteuil: white asparagus soup
Crème au Miroir: custard cream
Crème aux Groseilles: currant purée & cream
Crème Caramel: caramel custard
Crème Caramel à l'Orange: orange caramel custard
Crème Chantilly: whipped cream
Crème d'Artichauts: cream of artichoke soup
Crème d'Asperges: cream of asparagus soup
Crème de Champignons: cream of mushroom soup
Crème de Cresson: cream of watercress soup
Crème d'Ecrevisses de Burgos: cream of crayfish (lobster) soup
Crème d'Ecrevisses à la Joinville: cream of crayfish (lobster) soup with mushrooms, shrimp & truffles
Crème de Marrons: candied chestnut purée
Crème de Petits Pois Viennoise: cream of pea soup with capers, hard boiled eggs, olives & parsley
Crème de Tomate: tomato soup
Crème de Tortue: cream of turtle soup
Crème de Volaille aux Champignons: creamed chicken & mushroom soup
Crème Fondue: pineapple with meringue, nuts, apricot purée

Crème

& whipped cream
Crème Fraîche: heavy cream
Crème Française: caramel custard with whipped cream
Crème Printanière: whipped cream with puréed strawberries & strawberries in Kirsch
Crème Renversée: cold caramel custard
Crème Renversée au Caramel: unmoulded caramel custard
Crèmerie: dairy
Crêpe: thin pancake
Crêpe Bretonne: extra large pancakes
Crêpe Confiture: pancake with preserves & sugar
Crêpe de Homard: pancake with chunks of lobster
Crêperie: pancake restaurant
Crêpes à la Normande: pancake with sugared apple slices
Crêpes à la Russe: pancakes with preserves & meringue
Crêpes au Chocolat: pancakes with grated chocolate & chocolate sauce
Crêpes au Grand Marnier: pancake with Grand Marnier liqueur
Crêpes au Jambon: ham filled pancakes
Crêpes au Saumon Fumé: crepe (pancake) with smoked salmon
Crêpes au Roquefort: Roquefort cheese pancakes
Crêpes aux Fruits de Mer: pancakes with seafood in white wine sauce
Crêpes aux Oursins: pancakes with sea urchin
Crêpes Bretonnes: large pancakes with different fillings
Crêpes de Crabe Nantua: pancake with crabmeat, butter & cream sauce
Crêpes de Langoustines: pancakes with lobster tail & white wine sauce
Crêpes de Pommes de Terre: potato pancakes
Crêpes Flambées au Marasquin: pancakes flamed with cherry liqueur or pancakes with cherries & flamed with liqueur
Crêpes Parmentier: potato pancakes
Crêpes Roxelannes: pancakes with lemon soufflé & raspberry purée
Crêpes Soufflées à l'Orange: pancake with orange soufflé
Crêpes Souflées au Grand Marnier: pancakes with Grand Marnier liqueur soufflé
Crêpes Soufflées au Saumon: pancake with salmon soufflé
Crêpe Surprise Flambée au Kirsch: pancake flaming with Kirsch liqueur

Croustade

Crêpes Suzette: pancakes with Grand Marnier liqueur & flamed with brandy
Crêpinettes: sausage patty in pork fat with oysters on shell
Cresson: watercress
Cresson (Potage): leek & potato soup with watercress
Cressonière: watercress soup
Crevettes: shrimp
Crevettes à la Créole: shrimp with butter, rice & Creole sauce (tomato sauce with garlic, onions, white wine & Cayenne & red peppers)
Crevettes à la Danoise: shrimp with asparagus tips & shrimp sauce on croutons
Crevettes à la Diable: shrimp fried in Cayenne pepper & mustard
Crevettes au Beurre à l'Ail: shrimp in garlic butter sauce
Crevettes au Curry: shrimp with curry sauce
Crevettes Bouquets: shrimp in shells
Crevettes Grillés Meunière ou à l'Ail: shrimp broiled with lemon or garlic butter
Crevettes Gustave: shrimp in flameproof dish with asparagus tips, cheese sauce & grated Parmesan cheese
Crevettes Remoulade: cold shrimp with herb mayonnaise sauce
Croissant: crescent roll eaten for breakfast
Croquant: crunchy almond pastry
Croque Fromage et Tomate: grilled tomato & cheese sandwich
Croque Hawaiian: grilled ham, cheese & pineapple sandwich
Croque Madame: grilled chicken & cheese sandwich
Croque Monsieur: grilled ham & cheese sandwich
Croque Orientale: grilled ham & cheese sandwich with spices
Croque Orientale Oeuf: grilled ham, cheese & egg sandwich with spices
Croquets: almond biscuits
Croquettes: deep fried chopped meat, fowl or fish
Croquettes de Riz: deep fried rice croquettes with custard sauce
Croquettes de Volaille Truffées: chicken croquettes with truffles
Crottins: tiny disks of goat's cheese
Croustade: pastry shell
Croustade Agnes Sorrel: pastry shell with chicken forcemeat, mushrooms, ox tongue & German sauce (veal broth

Croustade

with white wine, mushrooms, egg yolks & lemon juice)
Croustade à la Nantaise: pastry shell with whitefish, mushrooms & tomato sauce
Croustade à l'Andalouse: pastry shell with rice, red peppers, chicken, eggplant & supreme sauce (veal broth with mushrooms, cream & butter)
Croustade à la Piémontaise: pastry shell with chicken, truffles & veal dumplings
Croustade à la Royale: pastry shell with cockscombs, kidneys, calf's sweetbreads, mushrooms, truffles & supreme sauce (veal broth with mushrooms, cream & butter)
Croustade Condé: pastry shell with calf's sweetbreads, mushrooms & truffle sauce
Croustade Copacabana: pastry shell with potatoes, turkey, bananas, sweet potatoes, pepper sauce & almonds
Croustade de Fruits de Mer: pastry shell with various seafood
Croustade de Saumon au Champagne: creamed salmon in champagne sauce & pastry shells
Croustade Nantua: pastry shell with crayfish tails (lobster) & truffles with Nantua sauce (white sauce with crayfish butter)
Croûtes: fried bread slices with various fillings
Croûtes à la Moëlle: bread slices with ox marrow & truffles in red wine sauce
Croûtes à l'Anglaise: fried bread slices with fish paste
Croûtes à la Norvégienne: fried bread slices with anchovies, truffles, eggs, salmon & chives
Croûtes à la Polonaise: fried bread slices with roast rabbit, anchovies & egg yolk with brown sauce
Croûtes à l'Epicurienne: fried bread slices with spinach, eggs, anchovies & capers
Croûtes à l'Indienne: fried bread slices with curried rice, eggs, shrimp & chutney
Croûtes au Foie Gras: fried bread slices with duck or goose liver
Croûtes aux Champignons: fried bread slices with creamed mushrooms
Croûtes aux Gourmands: open faced grilled ham & cheese sandwich
Croûtes aux Morilles: fried bread slices with creamed mushrooms
Croûtes de Champignons de Ségovia: fried bread slices with mushrooms
Croûtes de Moëlle à la Crème: fried bread slices with

Darne

creamed marrow
Croûtes du Gourmet: fried rye bread slices with ham & Swiss cheese.
Croûtes Méphisto: fried bread slices with carp eggs in hot sauce
Croutes Mirabeau: fried bread slices with anchovies
Croûtes Romanow: fried bread slices with puréed tuna fish & pistachios
Croûtes Rosamond: fried bread slices with tomato salad, anchovies & eggs
Cru Chou: raw cabbage
Crudités: raw vegetables with oil & vinegar dressing
Crudités de Saison: raw vegetables in season with vinaigrette dressing
Crustacés: shellfish
Crustacés à la Crème: creamed shellfish
Cuisses de Grenouille: frog's legs
Cuisses de Grenouille au Beurre a l'Ail: frog's legs in garlic butter
Cuisses de Grenouille aux Herbes Fines: frog's legs with finely chopped herbs
Cuisses et Rables de Lapin Dijonnaise: saddle of rabbit with Dijon mustard & heavy cream
Cuissot de Chevreuil: venison with chestnuts
Cul de Veau: veal rump
Cul de Lapereau à la Moutarde: rump of rabbit with mustard sauce
Culotte de Boeuf: end of sirloin of beef
Cultivateur: soup of carrots, turnips, leeks, onions, potatoes & bacon
Cumberland: sauce for meats of currant jelly, port wine, orange rinds & candied cherries
Cygne Royal: cream puff pastry shaped into swan forms with fluffy cream
Dacquoise: nutted meringue with butter cream & sugar
Dame Blanche: peach in syrup with vanilla ice cream & pineapple in Kirsch
Darblay: potato soup with vegetables
Darioles de Ris de Veau à l'Ancienne: puff pastry with veal sweetbreads, cockscombs, kidneys, truffles, mushrooms in cream sauce with chicken pieces & Madeira wine
Darne de Saumon au Champagne: slices of salmon in champagne sauce
Darne de Turbot Rôtie aux Aromates: turbot steak baked

Date

with aromatic spices
Date de Perdrix Rouges: truffled partridge pâté
Datte: date
Daube: braised beef stew in casserole
Daube de Charolais Nivernaise: beef in stock & red wine with carrots, turnips, onions & potatoes
Daube de Lapin: pieces of rabbit with pork skin, herbs & white wine
Daube de Vin Cuit et Cognac: beef in wine & flamed with cognac
Daube d'Oie au Vieux Buzet: goose with red wine, salt pork, onions, carrots & herbs
d'Auber: garnish for steaks
d'Augusta: garnish for fish in white wine
d'Aulagnier: clear beef soup
d'Aumale: scrambled eggs with ox tongue
Daurade: sea bream (fish)
Daurade à la Provençale: sea bream with tomatoes & garlic sauce
Daurade à la Sauge: sea bream with sage
Daurade Flambée au Fenouil: flamed sea bream with fennel (licorice flavored herb)
Daurade Grillée aux Herbes: sea bream grilled with herbs
Daurade Hollandaise ou Bonne Femme: sea bream with Hollandaise sauce (egg yolk, butter & lemon sauce) OR sea bream casserole with onions, mushrooms & bacon
Daurade Royale: sea bream with tiny egg custards
Délice Aubergade: delights of the Aubergade region
Délice Champenois: French cheese from the Champagne region
Délice de Brochet: pike delicacies
Délice de Sole aux Truffes: sole delicacy with truffles
Délice de Veau au Foie Gras: filet of veal with liver pâté
Délice du Château: delicacies of the chateau
Délice du Cyrano: duck broth with dumplings in white wine sauce & grated cheese
Délices de Bourgogne: snails with mushrooms & walnuts
Délices de Filet de Sole au Cliquot: filet of sole with champagne
Délices de Langoustines: small lobsters with herbed mayonnaise
Délices de Sole: filet of sole delicacy
Délices du Périgord en Brioche: truffles in yeast bread cake
Délices St. Pierre avec sa Mousseline: salt water fish with its

Double

own mousse & whipped cream
Délicieuses au Chocolat: chocolate delights
Demi Ananas Club de la Casserole: half pineapple casserole
Demi Coquelet au Curry: half curried chicken
Demi Coquelet Grand Palais: half spring chicken
Demi Coquelet Grillé, Pommes Frites: half broiled chicken with french fries
Demie: half liter of beer
Demi Glace: rich brown sauce
Demi Tasse: expresso coffee
Demi Sel: cream cheese
Demoiselles de Cherbourg: small lobsters
Demoiselles en Brochette: skewered lobsters
Dentelles: thin crisp pancakes
Denier, en: potato crisps
Dessert au Choix: your choice of dessert
Deux Cailles en Cocotte Paysanne: 2 quail in casserole
Deux Cervelles d'Agneau Meunière: 2 lamb brains in lemon butter
Deux Filets de Sole aux Queues de Langoustines: 2 filets of sole with Danish lobster tails
Diable: sauce of shallots, white wine, vinegar & finely chopped herbs
Diable de Mer: devil fish
Dinde: turkey
Dinde Farcie: stuffed turkey with onions, chestnuts & brown sauce
Dinde Rôtie: roast turkey
Dindonneau: young turkey
Dindonneau aux Marrons: stuffed roast young turkey with chestnuts
Dijonnaise: mustard sauce
Dodine: roast poultry or meat stuffing
Dodine de Canard Morvandiote: stuffed boned roast duck marinated with brandy
Dodine de Canard Truffée à la Facon de Fernand Point: boned duck with truffles & pistachios
Dodine de Canard Vieille France: duck in red wine
Dodine de Caneton Truffée: boned stuffed duck with truffles
Dolce Borghèse: sweet pastry
Dorade Grillée au Coulis de Tomate et Pistou: broiled sea bream with tomato juice, herb cheese, oil, garlic & spices
Double de Lapin à la Moutarde: hind legs of rabbit with mustard

Doucette

Doucette: corn salad
Doyenné: pear
Dragées: sugared almonds
Drupe: unpitted fruit
Duckling à l'Albuféra: roast duckling with ham slices
Duxelles: preparation of mushrooms, onions, shallots & parsley in butter
Eau Minérale: mineral water
Echalote: shallots
Echine: shoulder
Echine de Porc: spare ribs
Eclair: pastry with cream & icing
Eclair au Jambon: ham in cream puff pastry
Eclairs au Café, Chocolat, etc.: pastries with coffee, chocolate, etc. creams
Eclairs au Chocolat: pastry with chocolate cream
Eclairs au Moka: pastry with coffee flavored cream
Ecrevisses: crayfish (lobster)
Ecrevisses à la Crème: creamed lobster
Ecrevisses à la Fine Champagne: lobster in cognac sauce
Ecrevisses à l'Américaine: lobster broiled with butter
Ecrevisses à la Nage: boiled lobster with carrots, celery, onions, parsley, thyme, shallots, white wine & fish stock
Ecrevisses au Cognac: lobster in cognac
Ecrevisses au Pistou: lobster with oil, basil, hot soup, grated cheese & garlic sauce
Ecrevisses au Pouilly: lobster in white wine
Ecrevisses au Traminer: lobster in German wine
Ecrevisses au Vin Nature: lobster in wine
Ecrevisses aux Aromates: lobster with aromatic spices
Ecrevisses Bordelaise: lobster in white wine & herb stock sauce
Ecrevisses Cardinal: shells with lobster & Cardinal sauce (white sauce with Cayenne pepper)
Ecrevisses du Capitaine: the Captain's lobster
Ecrevisses en Salade: lobster salad
Ecrevisses Flambées aux Herbes de Sidobre: flaming lobster with herbs
Ecrevisses Flambées au Wiskey: lobster flamed in whiskey
Ecrevisses Georgette: potato skins filled with lobster tails, grated cheese & cream & crayfish butter sauce
Ecrevisses Newburg: lobster in Newburg sauce (cream sauce)
Ecrevisses Sauce Newburg: lobster in Newburg sauce

Epaule

(cream sauce)
Ecrevisses Sautées: sautéed lobster
Ecrevisses Suprême au Champagne: lobster in champagne, truffle & cream sauce
Ecureuil: squirrel
Egg à la Russe: hard boiled egg with caviar & mayonnaise
Eglefin: haddock
Eglefin Fumé: smoked haddock
Emincé de Foie de Veau Sauté: thin slices of sautéed calf's liver
Emincé de Veau aux Champignons à la Crème: thin slices of veal with creamed mushrooms
Emincé de Veau Zuricoise: minced veal with mushrooms in cream sauce
Emmental: hard cheese
Empereur: swordfish
en Brochette: on skewers
en Cocotte: in casseroles
Encornet: stuffed baby squid in sauce
Endives Meunière: endives sautéed in butter with broth & spices or endives sautéed in lemon butter
Entrailles: innards
Entrecôte: sirloin steak or rib steak
Entrecôte à la Moëlle: sirloin steak with marrow
Entrecôte à la Moëlle au Fleurie: sirloin steak with marrow & tomatoes stuffed with assorted vegetables
Entrecôte Bénédictine: rib steak with Bénédictine brandy
Entrecôte Bordelaise: rib steak with red wine & shallot sauce
Entrecôte Double aux Chanterelles: double serving of sirloin steak with mushrooms
Entrecôte Grillée: broiled sirloin steak
Entrecôte Marchand de Vin: sirloin steak with onions, mushrooms & marrow in red burgundy
Entrecôte Mexicaine: Mexican style sirloin steak
Entrecôte Minute Pommes Frites: minute steak & french fries
Entrecôte, Sauce Beaujolais: sautéed sirloin steak in red wine
Entrecôte sur Gril, Beurre Maître d'Hôtel: broiled sirloin steak with butter, parsley & lemon juice
Entrées: meat dishes, fish dishes or main courses
Entremets: desserts
Entremets du Jour: today's desserts
Epaule: shoulder of pork or mutton

Epaule

Epaule d'Agneau: shoulder of lamb
Epaule d'Agneau Braisée: braised shoulder of lamb
Epaule de Mouton: shoulder of mutton
Epaule de Mouton à la Boulangère: shoulder of lamb with potatoes, onions & stock
Epaule de Mouton au Riz: shoulder of lamb with garlic, rice & beans with red wine
Epaule de Mouton Farcie: stuffed shoulder of mutton
Epaule de Mouton Tourangeue: stuffed shoulder of lamb with onions & mushrooms
Epaule de Veau: veal shoulder
Eperlans: smelts
Epices: spices
Epigrammes de Poulet Lorraine: chicken breast with mushrooms & brown sauce
Epinards: spinach
Epinards à la Crème: chopped creamed spinach
Epinards à la Florentine: spinach with Mornay sauce (creamy cheese sauce) & grated cheese
Epinards à l'Ail: spinach with garlic butter
Epinards à l'Allemande: spinach in butter with onions, bread crumbs & brown sauce
Epinards à l'Américaine: spinach with lemon, butter & hard boiled eggs
Epinards à la Romaine: spinach with anchovy filets
Epinards au Gratin: spinach with bread crumbs & grated cheese
Epinards aux Cèpes: spinach with mushrooms & grated cheese
Epinards en Branches: whole cooked spinach
Epinards en Branches Sautés au Beurre: whole spinach leaves sautéed in butter
Epinards Purée: creamed spinach
Epis de Mais Poché: poached corn on the cob
Epoisses: cow's milk cheese
Equille: sand eel
Erable: pastry shell with creamy maple syrup
Erce: cow's milk cheese
Ermite: boar
Escalope: cutlet or thin slice of meat or fish
Escalope à la Chasseur: veal cutlet with mushrooms, shallots, tomatoes & brown sauce
Escalope au Paprika: breaded veal cutlet in sour cream & paprika sauce

Escargots

Escalope aux Morilles avec Farçon Savoyard: veal cutlets in butter with dry vermouth, cream, seasonings & mushrooms
Escalope de Chevreuil en Paupette: deep fried deer cutlet
Escalope de Foie Gras Frais aux Truffes: fresh fattened duck or goose liver pieces with truffles
Escalope de Napoléon: veal cutlet on rice with pâté, truffles & Mornay sauce (creamy cheese sauce)
Escalope de Truite Saumonée à l'Estragon: salmon-trout cutlet with tarragon
Escalope de Truite Saumonée à l'Oseille: salmon-trout cutlet fried in butter with sorrel (lettuce like herb)
Escalope de Veau: veal cutlet
Escalope de Veau à la Hongroise: veal cutlet in sour cream sauce
Escalope de Veau à l'Anglaise: batter fried veal cutlets with ham
Escalope de Veau à la Russe: breaded veal cutlet in sour cream
Escalope de Veau au Four: baked veal cutlet stuffed with mushrooms, tongue, truffles & cheese in tomato sauce
Escalope de Veau aux Morilles: veal cutlet with mushrooms
Escalope de Veau Cordon Bleu: fried veal cutlet with ham & cheese
Escalope de Veau Panée: breaded veal cutlet
Escalope de Veau Poêlée: veal cutlet in casserole
Escalope de Veau Valaisanne: veal cutlet with cheese
Escalope de Veau Viennoise: fried veal cutlet
Escalopes au Marsala: veal cutlets in Marsala wine
Escalopes au Marsala ou au Citron: veal cutlets with Marsala wine or lemon
Escalopes de Dinde: small round pieces of turkey breast
Escalopes de Saumon à l'Oseille: thin slices of fried salmon with sorrel (lettuce like herb)
Escalopes de Veau à la Crème: veal cutlets with cream & mushrooms
Escalopes de Veau aux Laitues: veal cutlets with braised lettuce
Escalopes de Veau en Papillote: Veal cutlets in cooking parchment
Escargots à la Bourguignonne La Douzaine: one dozen snails in garlic butter
Escargots à la Choucroute: snails with sauerkraut
Escargots au Chablis: snails in Chablis (white wine)
Escargots aux Noix: snails with nuts

Escargots

Escargots Bourguignonne: snails with garlic butter
Escargots de Bourgogne: snails in shells with garlic butter
Escargots de Sivry: snails from Sivry
Escargots en Cassolette: snails in casserole
Escargots en Croûte: snails in pastry shell
Espadon: swordfish
Espadon à la Florentine: swordfish in white wine with spinach & cheese
Espadon à la Génoise: swordfish in red wine, mushrooms & caviar
Espadon au Beurre Noisette: swordfish in butter sauce with hazelnuts
Espagnole: brown sauce
Essence de Poisson: fish bones in fish stock
Estouffade à la Bourguignonne: beef stew in red wine with bacon, onions & mushrooms
Estouffade à l'Alsacienne: pork stew in brown sauce
Estouffade à la Provençale: beef stew in white wine with tomatoes, garlic & olives
Estouffade de Boeuf: beef in casserole
Estouffade de Boeuf à la Niçoise: browned beef with pork, olives, onions, white wine, garlic & herbs
Estragon: tarragon
Esturgeon: sturgeon
Etrilles: tiny crabs
Etuvée de Volaille Albuféra: chicken stuffed with rice, chopped chicken livers & truffles
Excelsior: cow's milk cheese
Faisan: pheasant
Faisan à la Bohémienne: flamed pheasant stuffed with pâté
Faisan à la Bourguignonne: pheasant with onions, mushrooms & bacon in red wine
Faisan à la Crème: pheasant in cream sauce
Faisan à la Georgienne: pheasant in orange & grapefruit juices with hazelnuts in brown sauce
Faisan à l'Alsacienne: pheasant with sauerkraut, goose fat & bacon
Faisan à la Normande: pheasant flamed with apple cider
Faissan à la Zingara: pheasant with tomatoes, ham, tongue & mushrooms
Faisan au Chou Rouge (Saison de Chasse): pheasant with red cabbage (during the hunting season only)
Faisan Chatelaine: pheasant breasts in Madeira wine jelly
Faisan en Cocotte: pheasant in casserole with mushrooms &

Feuilleté

butter
Faisan Farci aux Raisins: stuffed pheasant with grape sauce
Faisan Grillé: broiled pheasant
Faisan Jacques: pheasant stuffed with forcemeat
Falette (Poitrine de Veau Farcie aux Herbes): veal breast stuffed with herbs
Far: wheat flour porridge
Farandole des 40 Hors d'Oeuvres: display of 40 hors d'oeuvres
Farci Chou: stuffed cabbage
Farine: flour
Faux Filet Grillé Vert-Pré: broiled sirloin steak
Fécule de Mais: corn flour
Fécule de Pommes de Terre: potato flour
Fenouil: fennel (licorice flavored vegetable)
Féra à la Savoyarde: salmon-trout with potatoes & Gruyère cheese (like Swiss)
Feuillantine: puff pastry cake
Feuille d'Automne: puff pastry
Feuille de Dreux: cow's milk cheese
Feuilletage de Roquefort: puff pastry with cream butter & Roquefort cheese
Feuilles de Vigne Farcies: grape leaves stuffed with herbal rice
Feuilleté: puff pastry
Feuilleté au Cassis: black currant puff pastry
Feuilleté au Foie Gras Frais: fresh duck or goose liver in puff pastry
Feuilleté au Roquefort: puff pastry of Roquefort cheese
Feuilleté aux Morilles: mushrooms in puff pastry
Feuilleté aux Pommes Chaudes: apples in puff pastry
Feuilleté de Caille Brillat Savarin: soufflé of quail in puff pastry with truffles
Feuilleté d'Escrevisses: crayfish tails (lobster) in puff pastry
Feuilleté de Foie de Canard: ducks livers with butter & Madeira sauce in puff pastry
Feuilleté de Foie Gras Frais: puff pastry with fattened goose or duck livers
Feuilleté de Fruits de Mer: puff pastry with seafood
Feuilleté de Fruits de Saison: puff pastry with fresh fruit in season
Feuilleté de Homard: lobster puff pastry
Feuilleté de Langouste Nantua: lobster meat in puff pastry with crawfish butter cream sauce

Feuilleté

Feuilleté de Moules au Pineau des Charentes: puff pastry with mussels in wine or liqueur
Feuilleté de Ris de Veau: veal sweetbreads in puff pastry
Feuilleté de Ris de Veau aux Morilles: veal sweetbreads in puff pastry with mushrooms
Feuilleté de Rognon au Marsala: kidneys in puff pastry with wine
Feuilleté d'Escargots: puff pastry with snails
Feuilleté d'Escargots Champenoise: snails in puff pastry shell with cheese
Feuilleté de Sole Sauce Champagne: sole in puff pastry with champagne sauce
Feuilleté de St. Jacques: scallops in puff pastry
Feuilleté de Truffes et Foie Gras: puff pastry with truffles & liver pâté
Feuilleton Berrichonne: pork & veal in puff pastry
Feuillton de Homard, Sauce Nantua: lobster in crawfish sauce in pastry shell
Fèves: beans
Ficelle Normande: thin rolled pancake with ham & creamy mushroom sauce
Ficelle Picarde: broiled pancake with ham in white wine sauce
Figue: fig
Filet au Poivre Flambé: flamed pepper steak
Filet Charolais en Feuilleté: filet of beef in puff pastry
Filet d'Agneau en Croûte: lamb tenderloin in pastry shells
Filet d'Anchois: anchovy filets
Filet de Boeuf à la Brabaconne: roast filet of beef with potatoes, croquettes & Brussels sprouts with Mornay sauce (creamy cheese sauce)
Filet de Boeuf à la Dilpomate: filet of beef with bacon, truffles & ox tongue in white wine
Filet de Boeuf à la Gastronome: filet of beef marinated in wine & wrapped in bacon
Filet de Boeuf à la Gelée: cold roast filet of beef in jelly
Filet de Boeuf à la Hongroise: roast filet of beef with ham & paprika in Mornay sauce (creamy cheese sauce)
Filet de Boeuf à l'Arlésienne: filet of beef with eggplant, tomatoes & fried onion rings
Filet de Boeuf à l'Alsacienne: filet of beef with ham & sauerkraut
Filet de Boeuf à la Lyonnaise: filet of beef with onions in white wine sauce

Filets

Filet d Boeuf à la Provençale: filet of beef with stuffed tomatoes & mushrooms
Filet de Boeuf à la Régence: filet of beef marinated in white wine & wrapped in bacon
Filet de Boeuf à l'Oseille: filet of beef with sorrel (lettuce like herb)
Filet de Boeuf au Poivre Vert: filet of beef with green peppers
Filet de Boeuf aux Morilles: filet of beef with mushrooms
Filet de Boeuf aux Truffes: filet of beef with truffles
Filet de Boeuf Brillat Savarin: roast filet of beef with rice
Filet de Boeuf en Chevreuil: filet of beef with peppery red wine sauce, chestnut purée, & gooseberry jelly
Filet de Boeuf en Croûte: filet of beef in pastry shell
Filet de Boeuf en Croûte Périgourdienne: Beef Wellington with truffles & Madeira wine sauce in pastry shell
Filet de Boeuf Madelaine: poached filet of beef, artichokes & onions in brown sauce
Filet de Boeuf Sarladaise: roast filet of beef with truffles
Filet de Boeuf St. Germaine: roast filet of beef with carrots & peas
Filet de Boeuf sur Epée Flambé à l'Armagnac: filet of beef on sword flamed with cognac
Filet de Boeuf Tour d'Argent: filet of beef on potato croquettes
Filet de Canard Gras: fattened duck breast filet
Filet de Charolais à la Broche: filet of beef on skewer
Filet de Charolais à la Crème aux Morilles: filet of beef in cream sauce with mushrooms
Filet de Chevreuil Sauce Venaison: deer filet with sauce of venison, red currant jelly & peppery red wine
Filet de Lavaret Savoyarde: white fish filet with potatoes, Gruyère cheese (like Swiss), dry vermouth & cream
Filet de Porc Rôti aux Quetsch: roast pork loin with potatoes & prune liqueur
Filet de Saint Pierre à l'Oseille: filet of fish in cream sauce
Filet de Salers Mignonette: filet of beef with black & white pepper
Filet de Saumon Soufflé au Beurre Blanc: salmon soufflé with white butter sauce
Filet de Sole Amandine: filet of sole with almonds
Filet de Sole au Champagne: filet of sole with champagne
Filet de Sole Cardinal aux Ecrevisses: filet of sole with white sauce & lobster butter
Filets de Sole en Brioche: yeast-cake bread with filet of sole

Filet

Filet de Sole Maison: filet of sole in the style of the house
Filet de Sole Murat: filets of sole with potatoes & artichokes
Filet de St. Pierre aux Deux Sauces: filet of salt water fish with 2 sauces
Filet de Turbot: turbot (fish) filet
Filet de Veau: tips of veal tenderloin
Filet de Veau à la Moutarde: veal filet with mustard sauce
Filet de Veau Citron: veal filet with lemon juice
Filet de Veau Grillé au Bacon: broiled filet of veal in bacon
Filet Garni: filet with vegetables
Filet Goulasch Stroganoff: beef goulash with sour cream
Filet Mignon: small steak from the tenderloin of beef
Filet Mignon Choron: beef tenderloin with artichoke bottoms, green peas, potatoes & white wine, egg yolks, shallots, tarragon & tomato sauce
Filet Mignon et Champignons: beef tenderloin with mushrooms
Filet Mignon Poêlé: beef tenderloin in casserole
Filet Poêlé au Pinot Noir: filet in black grape wine
Filets d'Anguille Grillés Beurre Moutarde: eel filets with mustard butter
Filets de Canard au Citron: duck filets or breasts with lemon
Filets de Canard au Poivre Vert: duck breast with green pepper
Filets de Harengs Pommes à l'Huile: marinated smoked herring with potato salad
Filets de Maqueraux: mackerel filets
Filets de Perche: perch filets
Filets de Rascasse au Coulis d'Ecrevisses: hogfish filets with crayfish (lobster)
Filets de Sole: filets of sole
Filets de Sole à la Bonne Femme: filets of sole in wine sauce with mushrooms, parsley & shallots
Filets de Sole au Puligny à l'Oseille: filet of sole with white wine & mushrooms in Burgundy wine
Filets de Sole aux Ecrevisses: filet of sole with crayfish tails (lobster)
Filets de Sole aux Epinards: filets of sole with spinach
Filets de Sole aux Nouilles Fraîches: filets of sole with fresh noodles
Filets de Sole en Civet: stewed filet of sole
Filets de Sole Espagnole: filet of sole
Filets de Sole Grillés: broiled filet of sole

Foie

Filets de Sole Marguery: filets of sole with egg cream sauce
Filets de Sole Mornay: filet of sole with sauce of cream, egg yolk & cheese
Filets de Sole Walenska: filet of sole in fish fumet with crawfish, truffles, cream, cheese & lobster butter sauce
Filets Mignon de Porc Forestière: pork tenderloin with mushrooms in sherry
Financière: brown sauce with Madeira wine
Fines de Belon: small oyster chunks
Fines Herbes: chopped herbs: tarragon, chervil, thyme, marjoram, chives & parsley
Flageolets: dried beans
Flambé: flamed dish
Flambiche: fruit pudding
Flamiche: sweet pastry tart
Flamiche aux Poireaux: pastry tart with leeks, butter cream & spices
Flamique: sweet pastry tart
Flamri: pudding with semolina & white wine
Flan: baked custard tart
Flanchet: flank
Flet: flounder
Flétan: halibut
Florentine de Brochet: pike with spinach & cheese sauce
Flûte: long French bread
Flûte à Potage: roll served with soup
Foie Chaud aux Raisins: hot liver with grapes
Foie Confit au Vouvray: duck or goose liver cooked & preserved in its own fat with white wine
Foie de Canard à la Gelée: jellied duck liver
Foie de Canard Alexandra: duck liver with white sauce & truffles
Foie de Canard au Porto: duck liver in port wine
Foie de Canard Braisé: braised duck liver
Foie de Canard Chaud: hot duck livers
Foie de Canard Chaud aux Raisins: hot duck livers with grapes
Foie de Canard Frais: fresh duck liver from specially fattened ducks
Foie de Canard Frais aux Pommes en l'Air: fresh duck livers with apples or potatoes
Foie de Canard Frais aux Raisins: fresh duck livers with grapes

Foie

Foie de Canard Frais des Landes aux Pommes: fresh duck liver with potatoes

Foie de Canard Sauté aux Raisins: sautéed duck livers with brown sauce & grapes

Foie de Cerf: deer liver

Foie de Porc: pork liver

Foie de Veau: calf's liver

Foie de Veau à la Berlinoise: calf's liver in butter with apple & onion rings

Foie de Veau à la Bourgeoise: calf's liver with onions & carrots

Foie de Veau à l'Américaine: calf's liver in butter with bacon & tomatoes

Foie de Veau à la Moissoneuse: fried calf's liver with green peas, potatoes & bacon

Foie de Veau à l'Anglaise: calf's liver with bacon

Foie de Veau à l'Orientale: fried calf's liver with vinegar, sugar, brown sauce, grapes & raisins

Foie de Veau au Bacon: fried calf's liver with bacon

Foie de Veau au Vin Rouge: fried calf's liver in red wine

Foie de Veau aux Bananes: fried calf's liver with bananas in butter, flour & lemon juice

Foie de Veau aux Oignons: calf's liver with sautéed onions

Foie de Veau aux Reinettes: fried calf's liver with apples

Foie de Veau Bercy: broiled & buttered calf's liver

Foie de Veau Grillé: broiled calf's liver

Foie de Veau Grillé à l'Espagnole: broiled calf's liver, Spanish style

Foie de Veau Grillé au Bacon: broiled calf's liver with bacon

Foie de Veau Sauté au Bacon: calf's liver sautéed with bacon

Foie de Veau Sauté aux Oignons: calf's liver sautéed with onions

Foie d'Oie Frais dans sa Gelée au Porto: fresh goose liver in its own jelly with port wine

Foie Gras: goose liver

Foie Gras à l'Ancienne: specially fattened goose liver braised in cream sauce & port wine with onions, mushrooms & truffles

Foie Gras au Naturel en Brioche: goose livers in cake yeast pastry

Foie Gras au Torchon à l'Ancienne: home-made goose liver

Foie Gras Cru au Poivre: raw goose liver with pepper

Fonds

Foie Gras de Canard: fattened duck livers
Foie Gras de Canard Aux Chasselas: duck liver with white grapes
Foie Gras de Canard aux Raisins: duck livers with wine & grapes on fried toast
Foie Gras de Canard en Brioche: broiled duck liver in yeast pastry
Foie Gras de Canard Frais: fresh fattened duck livers
Foie Gras de Dinde: turkey liver
Foie Gras de Landes: goose liver
Foie Gras des Landes à la Gelée au Porto: goose liver pâté in port wine jelly
Foie Gras en Brioche: duck or goose liver pâté in yeast cake
Foie Gras Frais: fresh duck or goose liver
Foie Gras Frais d'Alsace: fresh duck or goose liver pâté
Foie Gras Frais de Canard: fresh duck livers
Foie Gras Frais en Terrine: moulded pâté of fattened duck or goose livers
Foie Gras Frais Maison: fresh goose liver pâté of the house
Foie Gras Frais Périgourdine: fresh specially fattened duck or goose livers with truffles
Foie Gras Frais Truffé: fresh duck or goose liver with truffles
Foie Gras Reinette: home-made duck or goose liver with apples
Foie Gras Truffé: goose liver with truffles
Foies de Volaille: chicken livers
Foies de Volaille à la Bordelaise: chicken livers with shallots, herbs & red wine sauce
Foies de Volaille à l'Anglaise: chicken livers with bacon, butter & potatoes
Foies de Volaille à la Paysanne: chicken livers with shallots, mushrooms, parsley & lemon juice
Foies de Volaille à l'Orientale: chicken livers with onions, garlic, currants, lemon juice & tomato sauce
Foies de Volaille aux Echallottes: chicken livers with shallot sauce
Foies de Volaille en Brochette: skewered chicken livers with bacon & mushrooms
Fondants: icings for cakes or very small croquettes
Fondants de Volaille Truffés: small chicken croquettes with truffles
Fonds d'Artichauts: artichoke bottoms
Fonds d'Artichauts à la Bordelaise: artichoke bottoms in red

Fonds

wine & demi glace (brown sauce)

Fonds d'Artichauts à la Bruxelloise: artichoke bottoms in white wine with Brussels sprouts mixed with ham & demi glace (brown sauce)

Fonds d'Artichauts à la Crème: artichoke bottoms with cream sauce

Fonds d'Artichauts à la Florentine: artichoke bottoms with spinach, butter, onions, garlic &anchovies

Fonds d'Artichauts à la Jardinière: artichoke bottoms with assorted vegetables, cream sauce & parsley

Fonds d'Artichauts à la Hongroise: artichoke bottoms in white wine with carrots, onions, bacon, mushrooms, red peppers & garlic

Fonds d'Artichauts à la Lyonnaise: artichoke bottoms in white wine & brown stock with onions & parsley

Fonds d'Artichauts à la Maraîchere: artichoke bottoms with onions, leeks, tomatoes, garlic, potatoes & white wine

Fonds d'Artichauts à la Milanaise: artichoke bottoms in flame proof dish with butter & grated Parmesan cheese

Fonds d'Artichauts à la Niçoise: artichoke bottoms in oil, white wine, shallots, tomatoes & anchovy filets

Fonds d'Artichauts à la Princesse: artichoke bottoms with asparagus tips, chicken dumplings & truffle sauce

Fonds d'Artichauts à la Reine: artichoke bottoms with chicken purée, truffles & supreme sauce (chicken & mushroom cream sauce)

Fonds d'Artichauts à l'Espagnole: artichoke bottoms with red peppers, butter, onions & demi glace (brown sauce)

Fonds d'Artichauts à l'Estragon: artichoke bottoms with tarragon sauce

Fonds d'Artichauts à l'Impériale: artichoke bottoms with asparagus tips & supreme sauce (chicken & mushroom cream sauce)

Fonds d'Artichauts à l'Italienne: artichoke bottoms in white wine with Italian sauce (white sauce with tomatoes & parsley)

Fonds d'Artichauts au Beurre: artichoke bottoms with butter

Fonds d'Artichauts au Foie Gras: artichoke bottoms with liver pâté

Fonds d'Artichauts aux Asperges: artichoke bottoms with white asparagus tips

Fonds d'Artichauts aux Fines Herbes: artichoke bottoms with demi glace (brown sauce) & finely chopped herbs

Fonds d'Artichauts aux Morilles: artichoke bottoms with

Fraises

mushrooms
Fonds d'Artichauts Bayard: artichoke bottoms stuffed with goose liver pâté & Madeira wine sauce
Fonds d'Artichauts Club des Cents: artichoke bottoms with liver pâté
Fonds d'Artichauts Colbert: deep fried artichoke bottoms with liver forcemeat & Colbert sauce (meat glaze with butter, lemon juice, tarragon & parsley)
Fonds d'Artichauts Dubarry: artichoke bottoms and cauliflower with Mornay sauce (creamy cheese sauce) & grated Parmesan cheese
Fonds d'Artichauts Farcis: artichoke bottoms stuffed with mushrooms & cream
Fonds d'Artichauts Lucullus: artichoke bottoms with demi glace (brown sauce) & Madeira wine with truffle purée
Fonds d'Artichauts Montault: artichoke bottoms in Madeira wine with ham, mushrooms & asparagus tips
Fonds d'Artichauts Mornay: artichoke bottoms with grated Parmesan cheese, butter & Mornay sauce (creamy cheese sauce)
Fonds d'Artichauts Soufflés: artichoke bottom soufflé
Fonds d'Artichauts Vinaigrette: artichoke bottoms with vinaigrette dressing
Fondue: melted Gruyère cheese (like Swiss) seasoned with white wine, Kirsch liqueur & spices for dipping various foods into
Fondue de Poulet Papa Bergerand: chicken fondue with spice sauce
Fournitures: creamed chicken
Forestière, à la: served with mushrooms
Fourme d'Ambert: blue cheese
Fourré d'Ecrevisses à la Nantua: stuffed crayfish (lobster) with crayfish butter
Fraise de Veau aux Girolles: membrane containing the intestines of the calf with mushrooms
Fraises: strawberries
Fraises à la Créole: strawberries & pineapple in Kirsch liqueur with Kirsch sauce
Fraises à l'Arlésienne: tart with vanilla ice cream, fruit & strawberries in Kirsch liqueur & apricot sauce
Fraises à la Royale: sweet rice with strawberries & jelly with Grand Marnier liqueur
Fraises au Champagne: strawberries in champagne with

Fraises

champagne ice
Fraises au Sucre: fresh strawberries with sugar
Fraises au Vin Rouge: sugared strawberries with red wine
Fraises Bristol: vanilla ice cream with strawberries & strawberry purée
Fraises Cardinal: vanilla ice cream with strawberries, raspberry purée & almonds
Fraises Chantilly: strawberries with whipped cream
Fraises de Veau: veal tripe
Fraises Femina: strawberries in Grand Marnier liqueur with orange ice
Fraises Gourmand: melon with strawberries in Kirsch liqueur
Fraises Lacroix: strawberries in Grand Marnier liqueur & cognac on almond ice cream with crystalized violets
Fraises Marguerite: strawberries in Kirsch & Maraschino liqueur with pomergranate sherbet & Maraschino flavored whipped cream
Fraises Melba: vanilla ice cream & strawberries with strawberry or raspberry sauce
Fraises Monte Carlo: strawberries in sugar with brandy, Bénédictine & whipped cream
Fraises Nina: strawberries in Kirsch liqueur with pineapple ice, whipped cream & strawberry purée
Fraises Plougaste: strawberries with whipped cream
Fraises Rafraichies: strawberries in Kirsch & Maraschino liqueur
Fraises Renaissance: strawberries in sugar & caraway seed with pineapple mousse, Kirsch liqueur & whipped cream
Fraises Romanoff: strawberries in orange juice, Cointreau liqueur & whipped cream
Fraises Sarah Bernhardt: strawberries in cognac & Curaçao liqueur on pineapple ice with strawberry purée & whipped cream
Framboises: raspberries
Framboises à la Crème: raspberries in whipped cream
Frankfort Pommes à l'Huile: frankfurter with potato salad
Friand Lyonais: pastry with sausage
Friand Sanflorin: pork sausage with herbs in puff pastry
Fricandeau: pork liver pâté
Fricassée Alsacienne: chicken stewed with wine, onions & mushrooms
Fricassée d'Escargots: snails stewed in red wine sauce
Fricassée de Moules: stewed mussels

Fromages

Fricassée de Petit Poulet et Ris de Veau: small chicken & veal sweetbread stew
Fricassée de Petits Gris: stewed snails
Fricassée de Poulet: stewed chicken
Fricassée de Poulet à l'Ancienne: chicken stewed in cream sauce with port wine, onions, mushrooms, puff pastry rosettes & truffles
Fricassée de Poulet à l'Estragon: stewed chicken with tarragon
Fricassée de Poulet à la Mode de Bresse: chicken stewed with white wine, tarragon & parsley
Fricassée de Poulet aux Morilles: stewed chicken with cream & fresh mushrooms
Fricassée de Poulet aux Morilles à la Crème: stewed chicken with creamed mushrooms
Fricassée de Veau à l'Oseille: stewed veal in broth with cream, onions & mushrooms
Fricassée de Volaille au Chiroubles: chicken stewed with red Burgundy wine
Fricassée de Volaille au Poivre Vert: chicken stewed with green peppers
Fricassée de Volaille au Vinaigre: chicken stewed in vinegar
Fricassée de Volaille aux Morilles: chicken stewed with mushrooms
Fricassée de Volaille aux Morilles à la Crème: stewed chicken in cream with mushrooms
Frites: french fries
Friture: fried foods
Friture Mêlée (Cervelles, Ris de Veau, Légumes): mixed fry of brains, veal sweetbreads & vegetables
Friture Mêlée de Poisson: mixed fried fish
Fromage: cheese
Fromage Blanc: like cottage cheese
Fromage Blanc à la Crème Fraîche: cream cheese with heavy cream eaten with sugar or fruit
Fromage de Brie: brie cheese
Fromage de Porc: jellied pork loaf
Fromage de Roi: cream cheese
Fromage de Tête: meat boiled, jellied, sliced & served cold
Fromage de Tête de Porc: pork meat boiled, jellied, sliced & served cold
Fromages de France: French cheeses

Fromages

Fromages de Provinces: cheese from the various areas of France
Fromages de Suisse et l'Etranger: cheese from Switzerland & foreign countries
Fruits de Mer: seafood
Fruits de Saison: fresh fruit in season
Fruits de Saison Selon Cours: seasonal fruits
Fruits Farcis Croisés au Porto: stuffed fruit with port wine
Fruits au Sirop: fruit in syrup
Fruits Confits: candied fruit
Fruits Givrés: fruit filled with sherbet
Fruits Rafraîchis au Marasquin: fruit with Maraschino liqueur
Fruits Rafraîchis aux Liqueurs: fruit in liqueur
Fumé: smoked
Galantine: preparation of poultry, meat & stuffing wrapped in cheesecloth & steamed
Galantine de Canard: boned stuffed duck in jelly
Galantine de Cochon de Lait: boned suckling pig stuffed with forcemeat
Galantine de Grive au Foie Gras: boned stuffed steamed woodcock with duck or goose liver pâté
Galantine de Volaille: boned chicken stuffed with forcemeat, pieces of ham, tongue & pistachio nuts
Galette: flat cake made of pastry dough
Galette des Rois: baked pastry with almond cream
Galichons: small almond cakes
Galicien: cake with pistachio nuts & icing
Galmafrée: ham stew with artichokes, pimentos, beans, peas, tomatoes, carrots & onions
Gambas: very large shrimp
Garbure Soup: bean & cabbage soup with goose, herbs & garlic on bread crusts
Garbure Basque: fava bean stew with potatoes, white beans & herbs
Garbure Béarnaise: soup with potatoes, string beans, cabbage, turnips, white beans, herbs & sliced goose liver or ham with cheese croutons
Garne de Colin Meunière: hake (fish) in butter & lemon
Garnitures: vegetables & other garnish
Gasconnade: leg of lamb with anchovies, garlic & brown sauce
Gâteau: cake with cream
Gâteau au Cointreau: cake with Cointreau liqueur
Gâteau au Grand Marnier: cake with Grand Marnier liqueur

Gâteau aux Amandes: almond cake
Gâteau aux Amandes à la Confiture: almond cake with apricot or raspberry jam
Gâteau aux Noix: walnut cake
Gâteau aux Prunes: cake in crust with sugar, butter & plums
Gâteau de Foie Blond de Volaille: chicken livers in cake
Gâteau de Foie de Porc: pork liver pâté with garlic & mushrooms in cake
Gâteau de Noël: layer cake with chocolate icing & butter cream
Gâteau de Pithiviers: puff pastry, cream & almonds
Gâteau de Poires: cake with Grand Marnier liqueur & pears
Gâteau de Savoie: sponge cake
Gâteau de Semoule Sabayon: semolina (grain) cake with light egg & wine sauce
Gâteau du Prélat: cake made for high ranking religious person
Gâteau Feuilleté aux Framboises: puff pastry cake with raspberries
Gâteau Glacé: cake with icing
Gâteau Honey-Moon: honeymoon cake
Gâteau Marjolaine: meringue nut cake
Gâteau Orange: cake with orange cream, apricot jam & orange topping
Gâteau Saint Honoré: cake with cream puff pastry with cream & caramel
Gâteau Saint Honoré Mille Feuille: thin cake with cream & raspberry jam
Gâteau Soufflé au Fromage: cheese soufflé cake
Gâteau Tison d'Or: cake with icing
Gaufres: crisp waffles
Gaufres aux Fruits: thin waffles with fruit & preserve fillings with powdered sugar
Gaufres de Bruxelles: American waffles
Gaufrettes: thin crisp little waffles with powdered sugar
Gayettes: flat sausage
Géant Rose: red-skinned pork sausage
Gelée d'Oranges: orange jelly with orange sections & Curaçao liqueur
Gendarme: pickled herring
Génoise: butter sponge cake
Germaine: chicken or meat broth
Germiny: cream of sorrel (lettuce like herb) soup with herbs & croutons

Gésu

Gésu de Morteau: sausage in Beaujolais wine with shallots & potatoes
Gex: blue cheese
Gibelotte de Lapin: stew of young rabbit with vegetables, herbs & red wine
Gibier: stew of fresh game meat OR game meat
Gigot: leg of lamb
Gigot à la Ficelle: tied leg of lamb roasted over open fire
Gigot à la Sept Heures: tied leg of lamb with ham & garlic in white wine in sealed casserole for 7 hours
Gigot au Poivre Vert: leg of lamb with green peppers
Gigot aux Flageolets: leg of lamb with garlic, hare, beans, pan juices, tomato purée & garlic
Gigot aux Herbes: leg of lamb with herbs
Gigot Bordelaise: roast leg of lamb with mushrooms & cream sauce
Gigot Boulangère: roast leg of lamb with potatoes
Gigot Braisé à la Lyonnaise: leg of lamb braised in butter, tomatoes & onions
Gigot d'Agneau à la Liègeoise: roast leg of lamb with juniper berries & flamed with Genevre liqueur
Gigot d'Agneau à la Menthe: roast leg of lamb with mint sauce
Gigot d'Agneau à l'Anglaise: leg of lamb with carrots, turnips, onions & caper sauce
Gigot d'Agneau Béarnaise: heavily garliced leg of lamb with Béarnaise sauce
Gigot d'Agneau Bretonne: roast leg of lamb with white beans, tomato & garlic
Gigot d'Agneau Provençale: leg of lamb with garlic & herbs
Gigot d'Agneau Rôti au Gratin Dauphinois: roast leg of lamb with potatoes
Gigot de Broutarde à l'Ail: leg of calf with garlic cream sauce
Gigot de Lotte: anglerfish poached in sauce or anglerfish slices
Gigot de Mouton: leg of mutton
Gigot de Mouton à la Bayonnaise: leg of mutton with mushrooms, pickled cucumbers & anchovy filets marinated in oil, vinegar, lemon, red wine & herbs
Gigot de Mouton à la Boulangère: roast leg of mutton with potatoes & onions
Gigot de Mouton à la Liègeoise: roast leg of mutton with juniper berries & Genevre liqueur
Gigot de Mouton à la Menthe: roast leg of mutton with mint

Glaces

sauce
Gigot de Mouton à l'Anglaise: mutton leg with carrots, onions, turnips, celery, peppercorns & caper sauce
Gigot de Mouton à la Polonaise: leg of mutton with sour cream & cucumbers
Gigot de Mouton au Riz: baked leg of mutton with rice
Gigot de Sept Heures: leg of lamb cooked for 7 hours
Gigot des Greves du Mont St. Michel: leg of lamb raised on salt marshes
Gigot en Croûte: boned roast leg of lamb in puff pastry with mushrooms
Gigot Limousin: boned stuffed leg of lamb with mushrooms, garlic, pork & veal
Gigot Prieure: roast leg of lamb with potatoes
Gigot Provençale: leg of lamb with garlic, herbs & spices
Gigue: leg of (usually venison)
Gigue de Chevreuil: leg of venison
Girolles: mushrooms
Gite à la Noix: bottom round cut of meat
Glace: ice cream
Glace à l'Ananas: pineapple sherbet
Glace à l'Armagnac: brandy ice cream
Glace au Chocolat: chocolate ice cream
Glace aux Cerises: cherry ice cream
Glace aux Fraises: strawberry ice cream
Glace aux Pêches: peach ice cream
Glace Coupe: various ice creams or sherbets with or without sauces
Glace Crème: ice cream
Glace Crème à la Vanille Noisette: vanilla ice cream with hazelnuts
Glace Crème au Cointreau: Cointreau flavored ice cream (orange liqueur)
Glace Crème au Praline: ice cream with burnt almond flavor
Glace Crème avec Mignardises: ice cream with cookies
Glace Crème Cassate: mixture of ice cream like neopolitan ice cream
Glace Crème Tranche Cassis: black currant ice cream
Glace Crème Trois Parfums: three flavors of ice cream
Glace de Viande: thick brown gravy or stock
Glace Royal: white icing
Glaces: ice creams
Glaces Assorties ou Sorbets: assorted ice creams or sherbets

Glaces

Glaces aux Choix: your choice of ice cream
Glaces et Sorbets Maison: ice cream & sherbet of the house
Glaces Tous Parfums: all flavors of ice cream
Glaces Vanille, Café, Chocolat: vanilla, coffee & chocolate ice cream
Godard: sauce of ham, onions, carrots, butter & champagne with brown gravy
Gougette: spicy flat pork sausage
Gougère: cheese flavored cake with Gruyère cheese (like Swiss) OR with cheese cubes on top
Gougeres Bourguignonnes: cream pastry shell with Swiss cheese
Gougnette: sugared doughnut
Goujonette de Mostelle Tartare: small fried slices of mostelle (fish) with tartar sauce
Goujons de Sole: small fried strips of sole
Goulasch à la Hongroise: Hungarian goulash (beef cubes in paprika sauce)
Gourmand de Volaille Fermière: chicken with carrots, turnips, onions, potatoes & celery
Gourmandise Brillat-Savarin: filet of veal with mushrooms
Graisse: fat
Gramolatas: fruit syrup sherbet
Grand Veneur: brown sauce with currant jelly & cream
Granité au Kirsch: Kirsch liqueur sherbet
Grand Succès Réservé: ice cream cups
Grapefruit: grapefruit
Gras-Double: tripe
Gras-Double à la Mode des Landes: tripe with onions, ham, shallots, tomato sauce & white wine
Gras-Double Sauté: sautéed tripe with lemon
Gratin: various food with grated cheese & bread crumbs
Gratin Dauphinois: scalloped potatoes with Gruyère cheese
Gratin Dauphinois Flanqué d'Alouettes: scalloped potatoes with Gruyère cheese & larks (birds)
Gratin d'Ecrevisses: crayfish (lobster) with bread crumbs & grated cheese
Gratin de Framboises: raspberries baked in flameproof dishes
Gratin de Homard: lobster with grated cheese & breadcrumbs
Gratin de Langouste: baked crawfish (lobster) with grated cheese & bread crumbs
Gratin de Langouste du Chef: lobster with grated cheese &

Grenouilles

bread crumbs
Gratin de Macaronis: baked macaroni & cheese with bread crumbs
Gratin de Moules au Bresse Bleu: mussels with grated cheese & bread crumbs
Gratin de Moules aux Epinards: baked mussels & spinach with grated cheese & bread crumbs
Gratin de Palourdes aux Epinards: baked clams & spinach in cream sauce with grated cheese & bread crumbs
Gratin de Poireaux: baked leeks with grated cheese & bread crumbs
Gratin de Poissons: fish with bread crumbs & grated cheese
Gratin de Queues d'Ecrevisses: baked crayfish tails (lobster) with bread crumbs & grated cheese
Gratin de Ris de Veau: baked sweetbreads with grated cheese & bread crumbs
Gratin de Ris de Veau aux Nouilles: veal sweetbreads & noodles with grated cheese & bread crumbs
Gratin de Sole et de Langouste: sole & crawfish with grated cheese & bread crumbs
Gratin de Turbot au Nouilly: poached turbot in dry vermouth with grated cheese & bread crumbs
Gratin de Volaille: creamed chicken with grated cheese & bread crumbs
Gratinée: with grated cheese & bread crumbs
Gratton: king size pâté with meat chunks
Grecque, à la: olive oil, mushrooms, artichokes & eggplant in court broth with wine
Grenadin: small slices of veal with bacon in white wine
Grenadin de Veau aux Trois Moutardes: veal filet slices with 3 kinds of mustard
Grenadin de Veau Orloff: veal filet slices with vegetables & potatoes
Grenouille: frog
Grenouilles à la Poulette: frog's legs in white wine
Grenouilles à la Provençale: frog's legs with garlic butter
Grenouilles Fines Herbes: frog's legs with finely chopped herbs
Grenouilles Frites à l'Amoricaine, à la Poulette ou à l'Ail: frog's legs fried with brandy, white wine, tomatoes & herbs OR frog's legs with chicken stock & egg yolks OR frog's legs with garlic butter
Grenouilles Provençale: frog's legs with garlic butter
Grenouilles Sautées aux Fines Herbes: frog's legs sautéed

Gribiche

with finely chopped herbs
Gribiche: mustard mayonnaise with herbs & capers
Grillade Bordelaise: various items broiled with red wine sauce, mushrooms, eggs, artichoke bottoms & potatoes
Grillade de Porc: grilled pork chop
Grillades: various broiled or grilled items
Grillades au Feu de Bois: mixed grill done over wood fire
Grillades Marinières: steak with onions in garlic & anchovy sauce
Grillades (Poissons et Viandes): mixed grill of fish & meats
Grillé: grilled
Grive: thrush (bird)
Grive à l'Impériale: roast thrush stuffed with goose liver forcemeat in brandy sauce
Grive au Foie Gras: thrush stuffed with goose liver pâté in Madeira wine sauce
Grives à la Parisienne: small thrushes boned, stuffed & sautéed
Grondin: gunard (salt water fish)
Groseille: currant
Groseille à Macquereau: gooseberry
Groseille Blanche: white currant
Groseille Rouge: red currant
Groseilles Rouges de Bar: red currant preserve
Grosses Fraises: large strawberries
Gruau d'Avoine: oatmeal used in soups with milk, egg yolks & butter
Gruyère: cheese like Swiss
Guigne: sweet cherries
Guirlande de Suprêmes en Gelée: chicken breasts in jelly
Hachis: meat & vegetable hash
Hachis à la Parmentier: chopped cold meat
Hachis à la Zingara: corned beef hash with fried eggs
Hachis à l'Indienne: hash with curry
Hachis au Gratin: hash with grated cheese & bread crumbs
Hachis de Boeuf au Cervelle de Veau: roast beef hash in tomato sauce with calf's brains
Hamburger: hamburger
Harengs: herrings
Harengs à la Boulonnaise: herrings in white wine with mussels
Harengs à la Dieppoise: herrings in white wine with carrots, onions & bay leaves
Harengs à l'Anglaise: deep fried boned herring breaded

Homard

Harengs à l'Esthonienne: pancake with salt herrings fried with bread crumbs & sour cream
Harengs aux Haricots: marinated herrings with bean salad
Harengs Bouffis: smoked herrings
Harengs Frais: fresh herrings
Harrengs Fumés: smoked herrings
Harengs Salés: salt herrings
Haricots: beans or dried beans
Haricots Blancs: dried white beans
Haricots de Lime: Lima beans
Haricots de Mouton: mutton stew with beans
Haricots d'Espagne: runner beans
Haricots Flageolets: Lima beans
Haricots Mange Tout: beans in the pod
Haricots Rouges: red kidney beans
Haricots Verts: green beans
Haricots Verts à la Lyonnaise: green beans with fried onions
Haricots Verts à la Sauce Crème: green beans in white cream sauce
Haricots Verts au Buerre: buttered green beans
Haricots Verts au Lard: green beans with bacon
Haricots au Parmesan: green beans with grated Parmesan cheese
Haricots Verts Fines Herbes: green beans with finely chopped herbs
Haricots Verts Frais: fresh green beans
Haricots Verts Frais au Beurre: fresh green beans with butter
Haricots Verts Sautés au Beurre: green beans sautéed in butter
Helville: mushroom
Hochepot: meat & vegetables cooked together
Hollandaise Sauce: egg yolk, butter & lemon sauce
Homard à la Bordelaise: lobster in red wine sauce with shallots, brandy & tomatoes
Homard à la Française: lobster & vegetables in butter, cognac & wine
Homard à l'Américaine: lobster in butter & olive oil with sauce of tomatoes, garlic, onions, white wine, cognac & spices
Homard à la Nage: lobster with sauce of white wine, shallots, cognac, tomatoes & cream
Homard au Champagne: lobster with champagne
Homard au Porto: lobster with port wine
Homard au Wiskey: lobster flamed in whiskey

Homard

Homard aux Aromates: lobster in court broth
Homard aux Herbes: lobster & herbs
Homard Cardinal: broiled lobster with crawfish butter & cream OR lobster with sauce of lobster juices, fish stock & white cream sauce
Homard Châtaigner: lobster with chestnuts
Homard de Bellevue: lobster with scallops & glazed with hot cold sauce
Homard de Maine au Porto: Maine lobster in port wine
Homard Demoiselle de Cherbourg: small female lobster
Homard de Notre Vivier aux Choix: your choice of lobster from our tank
Homard Drouant: lobster in white sauce with cheese
Homard en Coquille: diced lobster with mushrooms & cheese sauce on scallop shell
Homard Flambé: flaming lobster
Homard Grillé: broiled lobster with bread crumbs & butter
Homard Grillé à l'Estragon: lobster broiled with tarragon
Homard Grillé à ma Façon: lobster broiled my way
Homard Grillé aux Herbes: lobster broiled with herbs
Homard Grillé Beurre d'Ail: broiled lobster with garlic butter
Homard Grillé Bretagne: broiled lobster with white wine, celery, onions & cream sauce
Homard Grillé Flambé: broiled lobster served flaming
Homard Grillé Flambé au Cognac: broiled lobster flamed in cognac
Homard Mayonnaise: lobster in mayonnaise
Homard Newburg: lobster with cognac & cream sauce
Homard Poché aux Herbes: lobster with herbs
Homard Puits d'Enfer (Sur Commande Hors de Saison): lobster (on special order if out of season)
Homard Rothschild: lobster & mushrooms with sauce of cream, sherry & cognac
Homard Rôti: grilled or broiled lobster
Homard Rôti à l'Oseille: roasted or broiled lobster on sorrel (lettuce like herb)
Homard Rôti et Flambé Sauce aux Truffes: flamed lobster with truffle sauce
Homard Sauté: lobster sautéed in butter & herbs
Homards et Langoustes Grillés: broiled lobster & crawfish
Homard Thermidor: lobster chunks with mustard, grated Parmesan cheese & sauce Bercy (white wine, shallots, parsley fish cream stock)
Hors d'Oeuvres au Choix: choice of hors d'oeuvres

Jambon

Hors d'Oeuvres des Gourmets-Deux Personnes: gourmet appetizers for 2 people
Hors d'Oeuvres Variés: assorted appetizers
Huile: oil
Huile d'Amandes: almond oil
Hiule d'Arachides: peanut oil
Huile de Maïs: corn oil
Huile de Noix: walnut oil
Huile d'Olive: olive oil
Huîtres: oysters
Huîtres à la Bouguignonne: oysters on half shell in butter, bread crumbs & grated cheese
Huîtres à la Florentine: oysters & spinach on half shell in cheese sauce
Huîtres à la Polonaise: oysters with ham & hard boiled eggs
Huîtres au Caviar: raw oysters in pastry tart topped with caviar
Huîtres au Foie Gras: oysters with duck or goose liver pâté
Huîtres au Gratin: oysters with bread crumbs & grated cheese
Huîtres au Natural: raw oysters on half shell
Huîtres Belon: oysters from Belon
Huîtres Bonne Femme: oysters with mushrooms, carrots, potatoes, parsley, shallots & white wine sauce
Huîtres Bourguignonne: oysters in red wine
Huîtres Farcies aux Amandes: oysters stuffed with almonds
Huîtres Fourrées: oysters with cream sauce
Huîtres Gratinées au Curry: oysters with curried cheese & bread crumb topping
Huîtres Natures: raw oysters on half shell
Huîtres Thermidor: baked chopped creamed oysters with Parmesan cheese
Huîtres Vertes: deep sea oysters
Hure: head cheese
Hure de Marcassin Truffée et Pochée: boned boar head stuffed with meat stuffing, truffles & pistachios
Igname: yam
Impératice, à l': sauce for fowl of duck pâté, truffles, mushrooms, dumplings or sweetbreads & wine sauce
Ile Flottante: meringue surrounded by custard sauce
Jambe: leg of meat
Jambe de Bois: clear beef soup
Jambon: ham
Jambon à la Charentaise: ham with Burgundy wine & cognac

Jambon

Jambon à la Crème: ham with white wine, veal stock & cream
Jambon à l'Alsacienne: ham with sauerkraut & bacon in Madeira wine sauce
Jambon à l'Os aux Aromates: leg of ham with aromatic spices
Jambon à l'Os Cuit Dans le Foin: leg of ham cooked in straw
Jambon au Cidre: ham in cider
Jambon au Four: baked ham
Jambon au Vermouth: ham in vermouth
Jambon Bouilli: ham boiled with onions & cabbage
Jambon Braisé à la Chablisienne "Papa Bergerand": ham in curry Chablis sauce
Jambon Braisé au Vouvray: ham with white wine
Jambon Chaud Demi-Sel: smoked ham with cream cheese
Jambon Cru: raw ham
Jambon Cuit à l'Os: ham cooked on the bone: sliced for hors d'oeuvres
Jambon D'Alsace à la Crème: ham slices with white wine cream sauce
Jambon D'Ardennes: boned smoked ham
Jambon Daugé aux Myrtilles: Daugé ham with huckleberries
Jambon D'Auvergne: Auvergne ham, raw or cooked
Jambon de Bayonne: raw cured ham from Bayonne
Jambon de Bayonne Melon: Bayonne ham & melon
Jambon de Paris: ham similar to U.S. ham
Jambon de Parme: Italian Prosciutto ham
Jambon de Pays: country smoked ham
Jambon de Poulet: boned chicken leg with Madeira wine
Jambon du Morvan aux Morilles: smoked salted ham with mushrooms
Jambon de Vivarais: thin slices of ham with mustard, pickles, bread & butter
Jambon en Croûte: ham in bread dough
Jambon et Melon: ham & melon
Jambon Frais à la Broche: marinated ham roasted on the spit with red wine & herbs
Jambon Fumé: smoked ham
Jambon Fumé Cuit dans le Foin: smoked ham cooked in straw
Jambon Fumé de Savoie: thin slices of smoked ham
Jambon Lacroix: ham sandwiches with goose liver pâté in Madeira wine
Jambonneau: picnic ham without bone
Jambonneau de Volaille au Pineau: large boned stuffed

Le Crêpe

chicken leg braised in wine
Jambonneau de Volaille de l'Aïeule: boned stuffed chicken leg braised in stock
Jambonneau en Croûte: picnic ham baked in bread dough
Jambon Persillé: ham with parsley
Jambon Rôti: roast ham
Jarret (ou Trumeau) de Boeuf: shank or knuckle of beef
Jarret de Veau: veal knuckle
Javanais: cake with apricot preserve & chocolate icing
Jésu: pork liver sausage
Joue de Porc Fumée: smoked hog's jowls
Jubilé: containing cherries
Judru: sausage of cured pork
Julienne: finely cut slivers of vegetables or meat to garnish foods
Jus: juice
Jus de Pommes: apple juice
Jus de Tomates: tomato juice
Jus de Viande: roast beef juices or gravy
Jus d'Orange Frais: fresh orange juice
Jus de Pamplemousse Frais: fresh grapefruit juice
Jus de Tomate: tomato juice
Jus Lié: veal gravy with arrowroot
Kaki: persimmon (fruit)
Kébab: skewered meat & vegetables
Kugelhopf Sauce Anglaise: yeast coffee cake with almonds
Kugelhopf Glacé: iced yeast cake in special mould
La Brochette de Poulet à l'Estragon: chicken on skewer with tarragon
La Cachuse: braised leg of pork with onions
La Caillette de L'Ardeche: tiny quail stuffed with liver pâté
La Cervelle de Veau aux Câpres: calf's brains with capers
La Confiture de Marrons: sugared purée of chestnuts
La Côte de Veau en Papillote: roast veal chop cooked in oiled parchment paper
La Côte de Veau Poêlée aux Endives Meunière: roast veal chop with endives in lemon butter & parsley sauce
La Coupe de Fruits Frais: fresh fruit cup
La Crème au Caramel: caramel cream custard
Le Crêpe de Crabe Nantua: crabmeat filled pancake in butter cream sauce
La Crêpe du Chef Gratinnée Crevette, Homard: pancake with cheese, shrimp & lobster
Le Crêpe Maison aux Fruits de Mer: house pancake with

Le Demi

seafood
Le Demi Douzaine d'Escargots: half dozen snails
La Fondue de Poulet Papa Bergerand: chicken with spice sauce fondue
La Galimafrée: ham stew with artichoke bottoms, pimentos, beans, peas, tomatoes, carrots & onions
La Glace Vanille ou Café: vanilla or coffee ice cream
L'Agneau du Tricastin Persillé: lamb with parsley
Lait: milk
Laitance: roe (fish eggs)
Laitance à la Cardinal: roe in pastry shell with lobster sauce
Laitance en Coquille: roe in white wine in shells with lobster sauce
Laitance en Gelée: roe in white wine jelly
Laitue: lettuce
Laitue au Beurre Noisette: braised lettuce in butter sauce
Laitue Farcie: lettuce stuffed with chicken or pork forcemeat
Laitues Braisées: braised lettuce
l'Alicot: stew of giblets, wings & bird with tomatoes, onions, garlic & kidney beans
Lamproie: eel-lamprey
Lamproie à la Bordelaise: lamprey with wine sauce
Lamproie au St. Emilion: lamprey with red wine sauce
La Mousse au Chocolat: chocolate mousse
Langouste: spiny lobster or crawfish
Langouste à la Ficelle Sauce aux Herbes: lobster tied with string & served with herb sauce
Langouste à l'Américaine: lobster flamed with cognac & sauce of white wine & tomatoes
Langouste au Porto: lobster tails with port wine
Langouste Belle Aurore: lobster tail with tomato sauce
Langouste en Sauce Estragon: lobster tails with tarragon sauce
Langouste Grillée: broiled lobster tails
Langouste Grillée à la Marjolaine: lobster tails broiled with marjoram (herb)
Langouste Grillée Cardinal: broiled lobster tail with lobster cream sauce
Langouste Mayonnaise: lobster tails with mayonnaise
Langouste Sautée: sautéed lobster
Langouste Thermidor: lobster thermidor (sauce of mustard, Parmesan cheese, white wine, shallots, parsley & fish stock)
Langoustine: tiny lobster or prawn
Langoustines au Champagne: prawns (small lobsters) in

La Poularde

champagne
Langoustines Flambées au Whiskey: prawns (small lobsters) flamed with whiskey
Langoustines Froides: cold small lobsters
Langoustines Grillées à l'Ail: lobster grilled with garlic butter
Langrés: soft cow's milk cheese
Langue: tongue
Langue d'Agneau: lamb's tongue
Langue de Boeuf: beef tongue
Langue de Boeuf à la Bourgeoise: beef tongue in red wine with bacon & carrots
Langue de Boeuf à la Diable: cold salted slices of tongue with mustard & butter
Langue de Boeuf Julien: pickled beef tongue in tomato sauce
Langue de Chat: thin flat biscuit
Langue de Mouton: mutton tongue
Langues de Mouton à la Nivernaise: sheep's tongue with onions & herbs
Langue de Porc: pig's tongue
Langue de Veau: veal tongue
Langue Ecarlate: salt pickled tongue
Langue Lucullus: ox tongue with truffle stuffed with chicken
L'Anguille Fumée: smoked eel
Lapereau: young rabbit
Lapereau à la Normande: young rabbit in cider with vegetables & herbs
Lapin: rabbit
Lapin Albicocco: rabbit with apricots
Lapin à la Bourguignonne: rabbit in red wine sauce with mushrooms, onions & croutons
Lapin à la Chasseur: rabbit in white wine & herbs
Lapin à l'Aigre Doux: sweet & sour rabbit marinated in wine vinegar with pickled cherries & chocolate
Lapin au Cidre: rabbit in cider
Lapin au Four: baked rabbit
Lapin aux Pruneaux: rabbit in red wine with prunes & currant jelly
Lapin en Gibelotte: rabbit in white wine
Lapin Frit: fried rabbit
La Potée Comtoise: salt pork, sausage, beef, mutton & vegetables on bread
La Poularde à la Crème au Champagne: roast hen in cham-

Lard

pagne cream sauce
Lard, au: with bacon
Lard de Poitrine: cured & smoked pork or bacon
L'Artichaut Vinaigrette: whole artichoke with oil & vinegar dressing
La Salade de Concombres: cucumber salad
La Salade du Chef: chef's salad
La Salade Verte de Saison: green salad with seasonal vegetables
L'Assiette de Cochonailles: pigs' tails, backbones & head with pickles & mustard
La Selle et le Carré d'Agneau Rôti: roast saddle & rack of lamb
La Sole Anglaise des Gourmets: English sole "Gourmet style"
La Sole Fourrée au Fumet de Meursault: stuffed sole in Meursault wine
L'Assiette de Crudités: raw vegetables with vinegar dressing
La Soupe à l'Oignon: onion soup
La Tarte aux Fruits: fruit pie or tart
La Tarte aux Pommes des Demoiselles Tatin: apple pie
La Tourte de Cailles: open-faced quail pie
La Truite de Rivière Meunière: brook trout with lemon butter
L'Avalanche des Hors D'Oeuvres: fish, vegetable, meat, egg & cheese dishes
Lavaret: salmon-like whitefish
Lavaret Glacé au Vin Blanc: salmon-like whitefish with white wine
La Vichyssoise: cold cream of leek & potato soup
La Voiture d'Entremets: pastry wagon
Lazagne aux Fruits de Mer: lasagna with seafood
La Caneton à l'Orange: duckling in orange sauce
La Caneton aux Cerises Flambé au Kirsch: roast duckling with cherries & flamed with Kirsch liqueur
Le Civet de Poularde de Bresse aux Vieux Beaune: chicken stew with red wine
Le Cocktail de Crevettes: shrimp cocktail
Le Confit de Porc: pork preserved in its own fat
Le Consommé: clear broth
Le Coquelet à la Moutarde: roast rooster with mustard
Le Pâté de Perdrix Rouge: truffled partridge paté
Le Demi Coquelet au Curry: ½ of a curried rooster
Le Demi Coquelet Grand Palais: ½ rooster
Le Filet de Sole Amandine: filet of sole with almonds

Le Poussin

Le Filet de Sole Meunière: fried filet of sole with butter-lemon sauce
Le Foie de Veau Grillé au Bacon: broiled calf's liver with bacon
Le Foie de Veau Sauté aux Oignons: calf's liver sautéed with onions
Le Foie Gras de Canard: fattened duck liver
Le Foie Gras de Dinde: fattened turkey liver
Le Foie Gras d'Oie: fattened goose liver
Le Foie Gras Sauté au Bacon: goose liver sautéed with bacon
Le Fromage de Brie: Brie cheese (creamy cheese)
Le Gâteau de Pithiviers: puff pastry, cream & almonds
Le Grand Succès Réserve: ice cream cups
Légume du Jour: vegetable of the day
Légumes: vegetables
Le Grenadin de Veau Orloff: braised veal filet with celery, lettuce, tomatoes & potatoes
Le Hochepot: meats & vegetables cooked together
Le Jambon Braisé à la Chamblisienne "Papa Bergerand": braised ham in curry Chablis sauce
Le Jambon de Bayonne Melon: Bayonne ham & melon
Le London Broil, Sauce Champignons: flank beef steak with mushroom sauce
Le Melon ou le Pamplemousse: melon or grapefruit
Le Napoléon: layered puff pastry with cream custard, jam & cake filling
Lentilles: lentils
L'Entrecôte ou les Côtes D'Agneau Vert-Pré: lamb chops with shoestring potatoes, watercress & lemon-parsley butter
Le Pigeon a l'Etuvée en Casserole aux Petits Pois Fins: pigeon casserole with green peas
Le Pintadeau Truffé: Guinea-hen with truffles
L'Epis de Maïs à la Crème: creamed corn
L'Epis de Maïs Poché: corn on the cob
Le Plateau de Fromages: cheese tray
Le Potage du Jour: soup of the day
Le Poulet de Grain Rôti aux Aromates et Pouilly: spring chicken with aromatic spices & white wine
Le Poulet en Civet au Vieux Bourgogne: stewed breast of chicken with onions, bacon & mushrooms
Le Poussin Poêlé Périgourdine: fresh young chicken in truffle sauce
Le Poussin en Surprise: boned young chicken in white wine

Le Rognon

sauce
Le Rognon de Veau Moutartier Flambé Grande Fine: veal kidneys flaming with cognac & mustard
Lepiote: parasol mushroom
Le Rougeot (Filet de Canard Sauvage Fumé): smoked filet of wild duck
Les Anchois Parmentier: anchovies, potatoes & dressing
Le Saucisson Chaud Lyonnais: poached smoked pork & veal sausage with hot potato salad
Le Saucisson Sec D'Arles: smoked pork-beef, red wine & spice sausage
L'Escalope de Veau Meunière: veal cutlet in butter with lemon juice & parsley
Les Champignons à la Grecque: cooked spiced cold mushrooms
Les Côtes de Porc Charcutière: pork chops in wine sauce
Les Crêpes de Volaille "Chanteclair": chicken pancakes
Les Crêpes Soufflées au Cointreau: crepe soufflé with Cointreau liqueur
Les Crudités: raw vegetables
Les Ecrevisses au Pouilly: crayfish (lobster) in white wine
Les Escargots de Bourgogne: snails in garlic butter
Les Escalopes de Veau au Madère: veal scallops in pepper, stock, Madeira wine & mushroom sauce
Les Filets de Sole Amandine: sole filets with almonds
Les Fraises: strawberries
Les Fraises au Sucre: sugared strawberries
Les Fruits: fruit
Les Fruits de Saison: fruit in season
Les Grenouilles Provençale: frog's legs with garlic butter
Les Hors D'Oeuvres Variés: assorted hors d'oeuvres
Les Moules Marinière: mussels in white wine & shallots
Les Moules Ravigotes: mussels in herb, cream, egg & butter sauce
Les Oeufs à la Mayonnaise: hard boiled eggs with mayonnaise
Les Oeufs en Tapenade: eggs in sauce of olives, anchovies, capers, garlic & brandy
Les Oeufs Pochés Bénédict: poached eggs on English muffin with ham & Hollandaise sauce
Les Pâtes: variety of pastries
Les Petits Beurres de Nantes: cookies from Nantes
Les Petits Pâtes: small varied pastries
Le Soufflé aux Framboises: fresh raspberry soufflé

Livarot

Les Quenelles de Brochet au Pernod et Estragon: pike dumplings with Pernod (licorice liquor) & tarragon
Les Salades de Saison: salads in season
Les Sardines Importées: imported sardines
Les Soufflés Tous Parfums: all flavors of soufflé
Les Surprises de Notre Patissier: surprises from our pastry chef
Les Tartes aux Fruits du Chef: assorted homemade fruit pies
Le Steak Dumas (Avec ou Sans Moëlle): steak (with or without marrow)
Le Steak au Poivre au Chambertin: pepper steak in Chambertin wine sauce
Les Terrines du Chef: chef's own terrines (pâtés)
Les Tournedos Rossini: little beef tenderloin tips in bacon & with liver pâté
Les Trenelles: lamb tripe with ham
Les Trois Filets: three (3) filets
Les Violettes Cristallisées: candied violets (flowers)
Le Homard Américaine: lobster meat with tomatoes, white wine, garlic, brandy & spices
Le Homard Bercy: lobster with white wine cream sauce
Le Homard Cardinal: boiled lobster stuffed with puréed mushrooms, lobster sauce, truffles with white sauce, grated cheese & butter
Le Homard de Maine au Porto: Main lobster in port wine
Le Homard Newburg: lobster meat in butter with cream, sherry, fish stock & egg yolks
Le Homard Thermidor: baked lobster meat with cream-wine sauce, mustard, butter & Parmesan cheese
Levraut: young hare
L'Huile d'Olive: olive oil
Liégeois: coffee or chocolate with heavy cream
Lieue Jaune: pollack (fish)
Lieu Noir: rock salmon (fish)
Lièvre: wild rabbit (hare)
Lièvre à la Royale: marinated hare with livers, vegetables & herbs
Lièvre en Civet: stewed rabbit in red wine sauce
Lièvre et Grives (Saison): rabbit & thrush (bird) (in season)
Lièvre Rôti a l'Aillade: roast hare with garlic & chopped liver sauce
Limande Sole: lemon sole (fish
Lingue: ling (salt water fish)
Livarot: soft, pungent cheese

Lobe

Lobe de Foie de Canard: duck liver
Lobe de Foie Gras Chaud Sauce Périgourdine: hot goose or duck livers with truffle sauce
L'Oie Farcie des Pruneaux: goose stuffed with prunes
L'Omelette au Choix: your choice of omelette
L'Omelette au Fromage: cheese omelette
L'Omelette au Saucisson de Pau: omelette with local sausage
L'Omelette aux Champignons: mushroom omelette
L'Omelette aux Fines Herbes omelette with green herbs
London Broil, Sauce Champignons: flank beef steak with mushroom sauce
Lotte: burbot or angler fish
Lotte à l'Américaine: poached pieces of angler fish in brandy, tomatoes, & white wine
Lotte Aurore: angler fish in butter & tomato sauce
Lotte aux Morilles: freshwater angler fish with mushrooms
Lotte Cardinal: angler fish filets in lobster cream sauce with truffles
Lotte Orly: deep fried filets of angler fish with parsley & tomato sauce
Lotte Sauce Gribiche: fresh angler fish with hard-boiled egg yolks, olive oil, herbs & egg white strips
Lou Magret: filet of duck
Lou Magret "à Ma Facon": duck steak "my style"
Lou Magret et Son Foie Gras Frais aux Raisins: duck steak duck liver with grapes
Lou Magret Grand Veneur: duck steak with brown sauce
Loup: sea bass
Loup au Fenouil: sea bass with fennel (licorice flavored herb)
Loup au Plat Provençale: sea bass with tomatoes, eggplant, mushrooms & garlic in olive oil & herb-wine sauce
Loup Braisé au Champagne: braised sea bass in champagne
Loup Braisé au Vin Blanc: sea bass braised in white wine
Loup Braisé aux Laitues: braised bass with lettuce
Loup de la Méditerranée au Fenouil: Mediterranean sea bass with fennel
Loup de Mer au Four: baked sea bass
Loup de Mer en Papillote: sea bass cooked in parchment paper
Loup de Mer Grillé: grilled sea bass
**Loup en Croûte Farci d'Une Mousse de Homard, Sauce

Manon

Loup en Croûte Sauce: sea bass in pastry crust with sauce
Loup Flambé: flaming sea bass
Loup Gourmande à la Mousse de Fenouil: sea bass with fennel mousse (licorice flavored herb)
Loup Grillé: broiled sea bass
Loup Grillé au Fenouil: sea bass with fennel
Loup Marin: sea bass
Loup Réserve Beaulieu: baked stuffed sea bass with wine sauce
Lyonnaise, à la: sauce of white wine, wine vinegar, onions & parsley
Macaroni: macaroni
Macaroni à la Napolitaine: macaroni with tomato sauce & grated cheese
Macarons D'Amandes: almond macaroons
Macarons de Boulay: macaroons with egg whites, almonds and sugar icing
Macédoine: mixture of fruit or vegetables
Macédoine de Fruits: fruits in heavy syrup, cognac or liqueurs
Macédoine de Fruits au Kirsch: fresh fruit salad with Kirsch liqueur
Macédoine de Fruits Frais au Kirsch: fresh fruit cup with Kirsch liqueur
Macédoine de Légumes: mixed vegetables with dressing
Mâche: corn salad
Mâche, Betterave: salad of lamb's lettuce with beets in oil & vinegar dressing
Madeira, (Sauce): brown gravy with mushrooms, meat juices & Madeira wine
Madelaines de Commercy: small sponge cakes
Madère: sauce of brown gravy with mushrooms, meat juices & Madeira wine
Madrilène en Gelée: jellied sherry consommé
Magret de Canard: duck steak (breast or filet)
Maison: house
Maitre D'Hôtel: whipped butter with cream, parsley, lemon juice & pepper (for steak)
Maltaise: orange flavored Hollandaise sauce
Manchon: small cake with praline cream in green almonds
Mandarine: tangerine
Manon: pastry dough baked & filled with cream, Kirsch liqueur, chocolate butter cream, apricot glaze & whole almonds

Maquereau

Maquereau: mackerel
Maquereau au Vin Blanc: mackerel in white wine
Maquereau Glacé au Vin Blanc: cold mackerel in white wine
Maquereau Vin Blanc: mackerel in white wine
Marcassin: young wild boar
Marchand de Vin: light sauce of red wine with pan juices
Mariné: marinated
Marignan: cake with pastry dough, rum syrup & whipped cream
Marinière: butter sauce with mussel juice
Marinière de St. Jacques: scallops in marinara sauce (garlic, tomatoes, parsley & anchovies)
Marjolaine: puff pastry & marzipan (almond paste) or oregano
Marmite: flameproof kettle-shaped pot
Marmite Dieppoise: fish stew
Maroilles: semi-hard, unskimmed cow's milk cheese
Marquise au Chocolat: rich chocolate cream with ladyfingers or biscuits whipped cream & jellied syrup
Marquise Crêpes: very thin pancakes
Marrons: chestnuts
Marsouin: porpoise
Martiniquais: cake with vanilla & chocolate butter cream, chocolate glaze, candied pineapple & cherries
Massepaïn: marzipan — small biscuits (cookies) made from almond paste
Matelote au Vin Blanc: fish stew with white wine
Matelote D'Anguille: eel stew with onions, herbs & red wine
Matelote D'Anguille au Vin D'Achois: eel stew with white wine
Matelote de Carpe: carp stew
Matelote de Fiélas: conger eel stew
Matelote D'Oeufs Pochés au Chinon: fish stew with poached eggs in red wine
Maubeche: sandpiper
Mayonnaise de Poisson: mayonnaise with fish
Mayonnaise de Volaille: mayonnaise with chicken
Mayonnaise, Sauce: oil, egg yolks, vinegar & seasonings
Médaillon: slice of meat from the tenderloin
Médaillon de Colin (Merluche) à la Romaine: small thick pieces of hake (fish) with spinach, potatoes, tomato sauce & gravy
Médaillon de Filet de Boeuf: filet mignon

Mignon

Médaillon de Foie Gras: toast with goose liver & truffles
Médaillon de Grive: thrush pâté
Médaillon de Lièvre au Foie Gras: hare terrine with liver pâté
Médaillon de Ris de Veau aux Morilles: veal sweetbreads with mushrooms
Médaillon de Ris de Veau Braisé: small, round nuggets of veal sweetbreads
Médaillon de Turbot à la Mornay: small, round filets or slices of turbot with Mornay sauce (cheesy white sauce)
Médaillon de Veau: veal filet
Médaillon de Veau au Marsala: slices of veal tenderloin in Marsala wine
Médaillon de Veau Prince Orloff: sautéed veal with purée of rice, cream, onions celery, tomatoes & potatoes
Melba: fruit & ice cream with raspberry sauce
Melon: melon
Melon au Jambon Cru: melon with raw ham
Melon au Porto: cantaloupe with port wine
Melon et Jambon: melon with Prosciutto ham
Melon Frappé: cantaloupe or honey dew on crushed ice
Melon Nature: fresh melon
Melon Rafraîchi en Surprise: melon with mixture of fruits & Kirsch liqueur
Menthe: mint
Menu Conseillé: recommended menu
Meringue: confection of egg whites with sugar
Meringue aux Fraises: meringue with strawberries & whipped cream
Meringue Belle Hélène: meringue with chocolate sauce
Meringue Glacée Chantilly: meringue with ice cream & whipped cream
Merlan: whiting (fish)
Merle: blackbird
Merveille: hot sugared pastry
Meunière: melted butter & lemon sauce
Meurette de Veau: veal in red wine, salt pork, onions, mushrooms & garlic
Mexicain: chocolate layers with apricot jam & chocolate fondant icing with nuts
Miel: honey
Mignardise: delicacies & dainty items
Mignon de Veau Braisé aux Morilles: braised veal tenderloin

Mignon

with mushrooms
Mignon de Veau Gratin des Capuchins: filet of veal with bread crumbs, cheese & capers
Mignonnette d'Agneau Gourmandes: slices of lamb tenderloin done to satisfy the big eaters
Mignonnette de Veau aux Girolles: small filet of veal with mushrooms
Mignons de Boeuf à l'Orientale: filet mignon with rice pilaff & curry sauce
Milieu de Tendron: cut of beef similar to the brisket
Millefeuilles: pastry with whipped cream & strawberry, apricot or raspberry jam with icing (Napoleon)
Millefeuilles à la Vanille: puff pastry with vanilla flavored whipped cream (Napoleon)
Millefeuilles de Jambon: ham puff pastry
Mimosa: sieved hard boiled egg yolks garnish
Minestrone avec Riz ou Pâtés: minestrone soup with rice or pasta
Mirabelle: kind of plum
Mirotin: beef stew with onions
Mirotin de Boeuf: beef stew in brown gravy
Mixed Grill Américaine: broiled beef, pork, lamb & liver
Mocha Cake: coffee flavored layer cake
Moëlle: bone marrow or brown sauce with white wine
Moëlle, à la: with poached marrow
Moka: mocha cake with mocha butter cream with praline & almonds
Moka Mousse: chocolate mousse with powdered coffee
Monsieur: mild flavored cheese
Mont Blanc: puréed chestnuts & whipped cream dessert
Mont Cenis: blue hard cheese
Montpensier: almond cake with rum
Morels: choicest wild mushrooms
Morille: wild mushroom
Morilles à la Crème: mushrooms in heavy cream sauce
Mornay: white sauce with Gruyère or Parmesan cheese
Morue: cod
Morue à la Lyonnaise: cod with onions
Morue Brandade de Morue: cod purée with oil & garlic croutons
Morue en Rayte: cod with onions, red wine garlic & tomatoes
Morue Farcie: cod stuffed with potatoes, eggs & oil in heavy cream

Mousse

Mou de Veau: calf's lungs
Morue Noire: fresh haddock
Morue Provençale: cod with garlic, olive oil & tomatoes
Mouclade Rochelaise: mussels on half shell stuffed with butter, flour paste, shallots & herbs
Moule: mould
Moules: mussels
Moules à la Crème: mussels in cream sauce
Moules à la Marinière: mussels in white wine sauce with shallots
Moules de Bouzique Farcies Marseillaise: mussels stuffed with fish forcemeat & crumbs with bouillabaisse like stock (fish soup)
Moules et Frites: mussels & French fries
Moules Farcies: stuffed mussels
Moules Farcies en Cocotte: steamed mussel casserole
Moules Gratinées aux Epinards: baked mussels with spinach & cheese
Moules Grillées: broiled mussels
Moules Marinière: mussels with shallots & herbs in white wine sauce
Moules Mouclade: mussels in curry sauce with cream
Moules Parquées à la Marinière: mussels in white wine & herbs
Moules Poulettes: steamed mussels in creamy white sauce with lemon parsley & mushrooms
Moussaka: ground lamb in eggplant skins with tomato sauce
Mousse: meat, fish or sweets puréed with egg & milk or cream
Mousse à la Constant Guillot: mousse of duck livers with cream
Mousseau: pound cake
Mousse au Chocolat: chocolate mousse
Mousse aux Framboises: mousse made with gelatine, raspberries & whipped cream
Mousse de Brochet: puréed pike with eggs & cream
Mousse de Brochet Nantua: pike mousse with cream sauce & crayfish butter
Mousse de Brochet Sauce Ecrevisses: pike mousse with crayfish (lobster) sauce
Mousse de Coquilles St. Jacques (Saison): mousse of scallops (in season)
Mousse d'Ecrevisses au Champagne: mousse with crayfish (lobster) in champagne

Mousse

Mousse de Faisan: mousse of pheasant with pâté & whipped cream

Mousse de Foie Gras: goose liver mousse with whipped cream

Mousse de Foies de Poularde à la Bressane: mousse of chicken livers with cream, eggs & crawfish sauce

Mousse Glacé: frozen mousse

Mousse de Homard Sauce Cardinal: lobster mousse with cream sauce with lobster juice & fish stock

Mousse de Rascasse à la Crème d'Anchois: hogfish mousse with cream of anchovies

Mousse de Rougets Champagne: red mullet & champagne mousse

Mousse de Saumon: salmon mousse

Mousse de Saumon Périgueux: puréed salmon mousse with truffle sauce

Mousse de Truite Richelieu: trout mousse with stuffed tomatoes, mushrooms, braised lettuce & potatoes or trout mousse with white wine, sherry, fish stock & truffle sauce

Mousse de Truite Saumonée: salmon trout mousse

Mousse de Turbot: turbot (fish) mousse

Mousse de Ventresca Gratinée: tuna mousse with oil, bread crumbs & cheese

Mousse d'Orange au Grand Marnier: orange mousse with Grand Marnier liqueur

Mousse Foie de Volaille à la Gelée de Xérès: chicken liver mousse in sherry jelly

Mousse Glacée au Moka et Nougatine: mousse glazed with mocha icing & nougat with glazed fruit & nuts

Mousseline: hot preparation of meat, fish or poultry with egg whites steamed or mashed potatoes

Mousseline de Brochet: very light creamy pike mousse

Mousseline de Brochet au Coulis d'Ecrevisses: pike mousse with puréed crawfish or puréed coral (fish eggs)

Mousseline de Brochet aux Morilles: pike mousse with mushrooms

Mousseline de Brochet Nantua: mousse made of pike & whipped cream with crawfish butter sauce

Mousseline de Brochet Sauce Diplomate: pike mousse with whipped cream & sauce made of fish stock, egg yolks, butter, cream, lobster juice & mushrooms with truffles & lobster meat

Mousseline de Grenouilles: mousse of frog's legs & whipped cream

Navarin

Mousseline de Homard: mousse of lobster, herbs & whipped cream
Mousseline de Jambon: mousse with ham
Mousseline de Langoustines Alexandra: pastry tarts with mousse, lobster tails, whipped cream, eggs & caviar
Mousseline de Loup: mousse of sea bass & whipped cream with herbs
Mousseline de Rascasse: hogfish & whipped cream mousse
Mousseline de Saumon au Beurre Blanc: light salmon mousse with sauce of butter, shallots, wine, wine vinegar & whipped cream
Mousseline de Saumon au Coulis d'Ecrevisses: salmon mousse with whipped cream & puréed crawfish
Mousseline de Saumn Joinville: whipped cream & salmon mousse with mushrooms, shrimp & truffles
Mousseline de Sole: sole mousse with whipped cream
Mousseline de Truite Flanquée d'Ecrevisses: trout mousse with whipped cream & crayfish (lobster)
Mousseline de Volaille: chicken mousse
Mousses en Gelée: various jellied mousses
Moutarde: Hollandaise sauce (egg yolk, cream & lemon) with Dijon mustard or Dijon mustard
Mouton: mutton
Mouton Chop: mutton chop
Mouton Chop Garni: garnished mutton chop
Munster: semi-soft strong cheese
Mûres: mulberry
Mulet: mullet (fish)
Mulet Rouge à la Bercy: red mullet with Bercy Sauce (butter & shallots)
Museau: muzzle or snout
Museau de Boeuf: beef head cheese
Mutton Chop aux Endives: grilled mutton chop with endives
Myrtilles: huckleberries
Mystère: moulded ice cream with hazelnuts
Nage, à la: method in preparing shellfish in court broth with herbs
Nantais: small almond biscuits
Nantua: vegetables & crayfish (lobster) in white wine
Nantua Sauce: purée of crayfish (lobster) with butter & cream in white wine sauce
Napoléon: puff pastry with cream custard & jam filling
Navarin: lamb stew
Navarin de Mouton: mutton & vegetable stew

Navets

Navets: turnips
Néapolitain: different flavored ice creams
Neige: chopped ice
Neige de Florence: flake-like pasta
Nélusko: petit four (cake) with cherries in brandy
Niçoise: salad with tomatoes, cucumbers, peppers, onions, hard boiled eggs, black olives, tuna fish, anchovies, salad greens & oil & vinegar dressing
Nids à la Chartres: fried bread with goose liver, hard boiled eggs & truffles
Noisette: boneless cut of meat
Noisette d'Agneau à l'Estragon: boneless cuts of lamb with herbs & brown sauce
Noisette de Chevreuil: slices of venison with game sauce
Noisette de Chevreuil aux Morilles: small round slices of deer meat with mushrooms
Noisette de Chevreuil St. Hubert: small round pieces of deer meat with sauce of game stock, lentils, mushrooms, sherry & tapioca
Noisette de Veau "Métropole": veal cutlets with artichokes in Béarnaise sauce (egg yolks, wine, butter, shallots, tarragon vinegar)
Noisettes d'Agneau: small round slice of lamb tenderloin
Noisettes d'Agneau sur Fond: boned filet of lamb on artichoke bottoms
Noisettes de Chevreuil: small round filet of venison
Noisettines: small pastry cakes with hazelnuts & whipped cream
Noix: nut or walnut
Noix d'Acajou: cashew nut
Noix de Coco: coconut
Noix de Veau: leg of veal steak
Noix de Veau aux Epinards: roast leg of veal with spinach
Noix de Veau Braisée: leg of veal steak braised with onions, carrots & herbs
Noix Farcie: sugar-coated stuffed walnuts & prunes
Noix Patissière: loin cut of veal
Nonnettes de Dijon: iced gingerbread cake
Normande, à la: cream sauce with fish stock, butter, eggs & cream
Notre Sélection de Glaces et Sorbets: our selection of ice cream & sherbet
Notre Terrine de Caneton à l'Armagnac: our baked paté of duck & brandy

Oeufs

Nougat Glacé: white caramel candy with nuts & glazed cherries
Nouilles à la Bolognaise: noodles with meat sauce
Nouilles Fraîches au Gratin: freshly made noodles with grated cheese & bread crumbs
Nouilles Vertes au Beurre: buttered green noodles
Nouilles Vertes Gratinées: green noodles with grated cheese & bread crumbs
Noques: dumplings poached in salted water
Nymphes à l'Aurore: frog's legs in white wine with paprika & champagne jelly
Nymphes Ballerines: frog's legs in jelly
Oeuf à Cheval: sautéed egg on top of hamburger
Oeuf à la Parisienne: shirred eggs on ground tongue & chicken with mushrooms & truffles with demi-glace sauce (meat & vegetable sauce)
Oeuf au Plat: fried eggs
Oeuf Béchamel: egg with white sauce
Oeuf Bordelaise: egg with red wine, shallots, marrow, pan juices & herb sauce
Oeuf Crème Fraîche: egg with fresh cream
Oeuf Jambon Fromage: eggs with ham & cheese
Oeuf Jambon ou Bacon: eggs with ham or bacon
Oeuf Lorraine: baked eggs on bacon & Swiss cheese with fresh cream
Oeuf Mayonnaise: hard boiled egg with mayonnaise
Oeuf Plate Nature: fried eggs
Oeufs: eggs
Oeufs a la Catalane: eggs with fried tomatoes, eggplant, garlic & parsley
Oeufs à la Coque: soft boiled eggs
Oeufs à l'Alsacienne: fried eggs with sauerkraut & ham
Oeufs à la Neige: poached eggs with meringues in custard sauce
Oeufs à la Tourangelle: poached eggs in red wine on fried croutons with wine sauce
Oeufs à la Tripe: hard boiled eggs with onion sauce
Oeufs à l'Espagnole: fried eggs with fried onions, tomatoes & sweet peppers
Oeufs Anchois: eggs with anchovies
Oeufs Argenteuil: egg with white asparagus
Oeufs au Four: baked eggs
Oeufs au Plat Bercy: baked eggs with sausage & tomato sauce

Oeufs

Oeufs aux Foies de Volaille: eggs with chicken livers
Oeufs Bénédictine: poached eggs & ham on toasted English muffin or bread with Hollandaise sauce (egg yolks & butter sauce)
Oeufs Bragance: eggs with tomatoes stuffed with sauce Béarnaise (egg yolks, butter, shallots & wine) & served with potato croquettes
Oeufs Brouillés: scrambled eggs
Oeufs Brouillés aux Asperges: scrambled eggs with asparagus
Oeufs Brouillés aux Truffes: scrambled eggs with truffles
Oeufs Brouillés Garniture au Choix: scrambled eggs with your choice of garnish
Oeufs Brouillés Hollandaise: scrambled eggs with Hollandaise sauce (egg yolks, butter & lemon)
Oeufs Choisy: fried eggs with potatoes
Oeufs Cocotte à la Crème: eggs baked in their own dish with cream
Oeufs d'Aumale: scrambled eggs with ox tongue
Oeufs de Saumon sur Toasts: salmon eggs on toast
Oeufs Durs: hard boiled eggs
Oeufs en Cocotte: eggs baked in casserole
Oeufs en Cocotte à la Crème: baked eggs with cream sauce in small casserole
Oeufs en Cocotte à la Reine: baked eggs with mushrooms, truffles & chicken base in casserole
Oeufs en Gelée: poached eggs in jellied consommé
Oeufs en Meurette: eggs poached in red wine sauce
Oeufs Farcis: stuffed hard boiled eggs
Oeufs Frits Mornay: sautéed or fried eggs with Mornay sauce (cream, egg yolks & cheese)
Oeufs Frits Tomate: sautéed or fried eggs with tomatoes or tomato sauce
Oeufs Froids à la Russe: hard boiled eggs stuffed with caviar & lettuce with tomatoes
Oeufs Jambon de Paris: fried eggs with ham
Oeufs Jambon de Pays: fried eggs with cured ham
Oeufs Mimosa: raw or cooked vegetable salad with hard boiled eggs
Oeufs Pôchés: poached eggs
Oeufs Pôchés Bénédictine: poached eggs on toasted English muffin, ham & Hollandaise sauce (egg-cream sauce)
Oeufs Pôchés en Gelée: poached egg in aspic
Oeufs Roses de Saumon: red salmon egg or red caviar

Omelette

Oeufs Soufflés aux Truffes et aux Scampis: truffle & scampi soufflé
Oeufs sur le Plat: fried eggs
Oie: goose
Oie à l'Agenaise: goose stuffed with prunes, pork, onions, green olives & eggs
Oie en Daube Normande: goose stuffed with pork, bacon, apples, braised vegetables & cider
Oignons: onions
Oignons à la Grecque: onions in olive oil & spices
Oignons Frits: deep fried onions
Oignons Frits à la Française: French fried onion rings
Omble: fresh water fish (char)
Omble Chevalier: char in wine sauce
Omble Chevalier au Beurre Mousse: char with whipped butter
Omble Chevalier au Champagne: char in champagne
Omble Chevalier Braisé Crème Wiskey et Morilles: char with creamed mushrooms & whiskey in cream sauce
Omble Soufflé à l'Oseille: char soufflé with sorrel (lettuce like herb)
Omelette a la Norvégienne: baked Alaska
Omelette au Choix: your choice of omelette
Omelette au Foies de Volaille: chicken liver omelette
Omelette au Fromage: cheese omelette
Omelette au Jambon de Paris: ham omelette
Omelette au Jambon de Pays: cured ham omelette
Omelette aux Champignons: mushroom omelette
Omelette aux Fines Herbes: herb omelette (parsley, tarragon, etc.)
Omelette aux Foies de Volaille: chicken liver omelette
Omelette aux Langoustines: omelette with sautéed lobster tails
Omelette aux Marrons: pancake style omelette with chestnut cream, another omelette, toasted nuts & flamed with Kirsch liqueur
Omelette aux Morilles: omelette with mushrooms
Omelette aux Pointes d'Asperges: omelette with asparagus tips
Omelette aux Truffes: omelette with truffles
Omelette Brayude: cream & potato omelette
Omelette Cardinal: omelette with lobster & orange
Omelette Clarmart: omelette stuffed with peas
Omelette Confiture: omelette with preserves or jelly & pow-

Omelette

dered sugar
Omelette de Homard: lobster omelette
Omelette de Homard Cancalaise: lobster omelette with oysters, shelled shrimp & cream sauce
Omelette de Langoustes a l'Amoricaine: omelette with lobster meat with choice of: truffles, corn fritters, fried sweet potatoes or sauce of lobster & lobster coral (eggs), white wine, butter & brandy
Omelette de Noix et d'Escargots: omelette with snails & walnuts
Omelette des Vosges: mushroom omelette
Omelette de Périgord (Truffes): truffle omelette
Omelette Espagnole: omelette with tomatoes, green pepper & onions in tomato sauce
Omelette Fines Herbes: herb omelette
Omelette Flambée: omelette with sugar & flamed with brandy
Omelette Fournée de Courgettes et de Tomates: omelette stuffed with slices of zucchini & tomatoes
Omelette Garniture au Choix: omelette made to your order
Omelette Lyonnaise: omelette with onions, chicken livers & truffles
Omelette Monégasque Chaude: omelette on tomatoes fried in oil with tarragon, anchovy filets & tomato sauce
Omelette Nature: plain omelette
Omelette Norvégienne: baked Alaska
Omelette Savoyarde: cheese omelette
Omelette Soufflée à la Liqueur: fluffy omelette with liqueur
Omelette Soufflée au Rhum: fluffy omelette with rum
Omelette Surprise: omelette with sherbet or ice cream
Onglet: strip encasing the ribs
Onglet de Boeuf: beef rib strips sautéed in butter & onions
Orange, à l': sauce for duck of stock, white wine, orange liqueur, orange juice & red currant jelly
Oranges à l'Orientale: oranges Oriental style
Orangine: cake with candied orange peel
Oreilles d'Agneau: lamb's ears
Oreilles de Cochon: sugared puff pastry or pig's ears
Oreilles de Porc: pig's ears
Oreilles et Queues de Porc Grillées: pig's ears & tail
Oreillons de Veau Farcis: stuffed calf's ears
Orphie: garfish
Ortolans Rôtis: tiny birds roasted in vine leaves
Osso Bucco: veal knuckle stewed with onions & tomatoes
Osso Bucco à l'Orange: braised veal knuckle with orange

Pannequets

sauce
Ours: bear
Oursinade: sea urchin soup
Oursins: raw sea urchins
Oxtail Clair au Porto: oxtail soup with port wine
Paélla: fish stew with shrimp, mussels, lobster, chicken, sausage, vegetables & rice
Päella Valenciana: assorted fish, seafood, chicken & vegetables on saffron rice
Pageot: fish similar to mullet
Paillardine (Escalope de Veau) à la Sauge: veal scallops with sage
Pailleté à la Framboise: raspberry puff pastry
Paillettes: pastry sticks
Paillettes de Fromage: thinly cut cheese pieces
Pain: bread
Pain Ambroisie: almond cake with candied fruits
Pain au Chocolat: pastry with chocolate bar filling
Pain aux Fruits: fruit cake
Pain Complet: almond pastry cake
Pain de Gênes: almond cake with Kirsch liqueur
Pain d'Epices: spice cake
Pain de Sucre: sugar loaf
Pain Grillé: toast
Paleron: chuck roast steak for stocks & braising
Palmiers: puff pastry cookies shaped like butterflies glazed with sugar
Palombe: wild dove
Palombes Rôties: doves roasted in vine leaves
Palourdes: raw or baked clams
Palourdes Farcies: stuffed clams
Palourdes Grillées Farcies: broiled stuffed clams
Pamplemousse: grapefruit
Pamplemousse au Crabes: grapefruit & crab salad
Pamplemousse au Marasquin: grapefruit with Maraschino liqueur
Pamplemousse Cocktail: grapefruit cocktail
Pamplemousse de Lévante: grapefruit from Lévante
Panaché: mixture of food
Panaché de Coquillages Frais: stuffed mixture of shell fish
Pan Bagnat: canapé with tomatoes, anchovies & olives
Panais: parsnip
Pannequets: filled pancakes
Pannequets de Ris de Veau: pancake with veal sweetbreads

Pannequets

Pannequets Grimaldi: pancakes with tomato purée or custard & strips of celeriac (celery flavored root)
Pannequets Soufflés Flambés: flaming soufflé pancakes
Paon: peacock
Parfait: mixture of eggs, seasonings & cream frozen in tulip shaped glasses
Parfait aux Foies de Volaille: chicken livers in a parfait glass or paté with whipped cream
Parfait de Foie Gras Frais: fresh duck or goose liver pâté in tulip shaped glass
Parfait de Foie Gras "Maison": house goose liver pâté in tulip shaped glass
Parfait de Foies de Volaille: chicken liver pâté in tulip shaped glass
Parfait de Ris de Veau Truffé: puréed veal sweetbreads with truffles in tulip shaped glass
Parfait Glacé: dessert of egg, cream, liqueur or ice cream & flavoring in tulip shaped glass
Parfait Moka: chocolate & coffee flavored whipped cream dessert in tulip shaped glass
Parfaits à la Liqueur: ice cream & liqueur with whipped cream
Paris-Brest: cream puff pastry with cream, almonds, almond paste & powdered sugar
Parmentier, à la: served with potatoes
Pastèque: watermelon
Patate: sweet potato
Pâté: ground meat, poultry or fish baked in crock
Pâte: various pastry doughs or pasta
Pâte au Four: baked pasta
Pâte au Saindoux: pastry dough for large cold pies
Pâte aux Tartelettes: pastry dough for tartelettes
Pâté aux Truffes: pâté with truffles
Pâte Brisée: pie crust
Pâté Chaud Beurre Blanc: liver pâté with hot white butter sauce
Pâté Chaud Bourgeois: hot pâté with red wine, carrots, onions & bacon
Pâté Chaud de Brochet: hot pike (fish) pâté
Pâté Chaud de Mostelle: hot pâté of fish
Pâté Chaud Roussotte: larks stuffed with forcemeat & spices baked in crust
Pâté d'Abatis d'Oie: goose giblet pie
Pâté d'Alouette: lark meat pâté

Pâtisseries

Pâté de Bécasse au Foie Gras: woodcock (bird) pâté with duck or goose liver pâté
Pâté de Brochet: cold pike pâté
Pâté de Brochet aux Mousquetaires: pâté of pike
Pâté de Campagne: country pâté
Pâté de Caneton de Rouen: boned duck with forcemeat & its own pâté
Pâté de Carpe au St. Amour: carp pâté with red burgundy wine
Pâté de Foie a l'Armagnac: liver pâté with cognac
Pâté de Foie de Canard Truffé Maison: house duck liver pâté with truffles
Pâté de Foies de Volaille: chicken liver pâté
Pâté de Foie Gras de Canard: pâté from livers of specially fattened ducks
Pâté de Merle: blackbird pâté
Pâté de Pithiviers: pâté of larks stuffed with their giblets & pork
Pâté de Poissons de Loire: pâté from fish caught in the Loire River
Pâté de Saumon Frais: pâté of fresh salmon
Pâté de Sole à la Mousse de Rougets: sole pâté with mousse of red mullet
Pâté de Sole à l'Oseille: pâté of sole with sorrel (lettuce like herb)
Pâté de Truite: trout pâté
Pâté de Volaille en Croûte: pâté of chicken livers in crust
Pâté du Chef: chef's pâté
Pâté en Croûte: pâté in pastry crust
Pâté en Croûte au Foie Gras: duck or goose liver pâté in pastry crust
Pâté Feuilletée: puff pastry with pie crust for long strip tarts
Pâté Froid du Patron: the boss' cold pâté
Pâté Maison: house pâté
Pâte Sablée: sweet rich crust like cookie dough
Pâtés de Grives: pâté made of thrush meat
Pâtes Fraîches aux Truffes: truffles in fresh pastry
Pâté Truffé Périgourdin: pâté made with truffles from Périgourd & goose livers
Pâtisserie Maison: house pastries
Pâtisseries: pastries
Pâtisseries du Jour: pastries of the day
Pâtisseries Françaises: French pastries
Pâtisseries Françaises Assorties ou Tarte aux Fruits:

Pauchouse

assorted French pastries or fruit tarts
Pauchouse: fresh water fish stew
Pauchouse Bourguignonne: fresh water fish stew
Paupiette à la Berrichonne: raw meat slices around sausage poached with vegetables
Paupiette de Bar au Coulis d'Ecrevisses: rolled fish filets with crayfish (lobster) sauce
Paupiette de Volaille aux Morilles: sliced chicken around sausages poached with mushrooms
Paupiette de Volaille Grand Veneur: rolled sliced chicken with red wine, pepper, red currant jelly, venison & cream sauce
Paupiettes de Dinde: rolled & stuffed sliced turkey
Paupiettes de Veau à la Façon de Rosine: braised veal scallops stuffed with forcemeat & herbs
Pavé au Chocolat: chocolate sponge cake with chocolate butter icing
Pavé au Poivre: steak with peppercorns
Pavé au Poivre Vert: beef tenderloin with green peppers
Pavé de Boeuf aux Morilles: cold beef with mushrooms
Pavé du Mail: square or rectangular dish
Pêau: skin
Pêche: peach
Pêche au Sirop: peach with syrup
Pêche Flambée: peach flamed with Cointreau
Pêche Meringuée: peach with meringue
Pêches Cardinal: whipped cream with peach halves, raspberry purée & chopped nuts on top
Pêches Flambées: flaming peaches with liqueur
Pêches Flambées au Sureau: peaches flamed with elderberry wine
Pêches Melba: vanilla ice cream with peaches & cassis (black currants) or raspberry sauce
Pêche Soufflée "Belle Compiègnoise": peach soufflé
Pellmènes à la Sibirienne: raviolis stuffed with hen & ham with butter
Perche: perch
Perche Noir: black bass
Perchettes: young perch
Perdreau: young partridge
Perdreau Farci Façon de l'Auberge: young partridge stuffed in the style of the "Inn"
Perdrix: old partridge
Perdrix à la Vigneronne: partridges with grapes

Pièce

Perdrix au Nid: roast partridge in artichoke bottoms
Pereau à la Normande: rabbit in cider with vegetables
Périgourdine: brown sauce with liver pâté & truffles
Périgueux: sauce of truffle essence & truffles
Perles d'Astrachan Béluga Malossol: Persian Beluga caviar
Perles Suisses: cream with Swiss cheese
Persil: parsley
Persillade: chopped parsley
Petit: little
Petit Déjeuner: breakfast
Petit Homard à la Nage: small live lobster
Petite Marmite: clear strong broth in casserole
Petite Marmite à l'Alsacienne: clear broth with onions, parsley & mushrooms
Petite Marmite du Pêcheur: baked casserole of various fish with broth
Petit Salé: salted belly or pork flank
Petit Salé aux Choux Braisés: pickled pork with braised cabbage
Petit Salé Aux Lentilles: salted pork belly with lentils
Petits Fours: small cakes, pastries & tarts
Petits Gris: snails in herb butter
Petits Oiseaux: small game birds
Petits Pains de Caviar à la Russe: toasted rolls with caviar, onions & chives
Petits Pâtés: fish, game or poultry patties
Petits Pieds: small birds
Petits Pois: little green peas
Petits Pois à la Bonne Femme: small green peas with onions
Petits Pois à la Française: tiny green peas with lettuce, ham & butter
Petits Pois Jambon: little peas with ham
Petits Pois au Beurre: little green peas with butter
Petits Pois au Lard: little peas with bacon bits
Petits Pois de Crème: little individual pots of custard
Petit Suisse: rich cream cheese
Petits Soufflés: small soufflés
Pétoncle: scallops
Pétoncles Farcies: stuffed scallops
Pets de Nonne: deep fried pastry with powdered sugar
Piccata de Veau: slices of seasoned veal with lemon juice, floured & fried in butter
Pièce d'Agneau en Casserole et à l'Ail: lamb rump roast in casserole with garlic

Pièce

Pièce de Boeuf à la Bouguignonne: braised beef rump roast in red wine, glazed onions & mushrooms
Pièce de Boeuf à la Moëlle: rump roast of beef with marrow
Pièce de Boeuf à l'Etuvée aux Olives: rump roast of beef in casserole with olives
Pièce de Boeuf au Poivre Vert: rump roast of beef with green pepper
Pièce de Boeuf Berrichonne: rump roast of beef with glazed onions, chestnuts, bacon & braised cabbage
Pièce de Charolais Sauce Moëlle: piece of beef with marrow sauce
Pied de Cochon: grilled pig's feet
Pied de Mouton Poulette: lamb's knuckles in cream sauce
Pied de Veau: calf's feet
Pieds: feet
Pieds d'Agneau: lamb trotters
Pieds de Cochon en Daube: pig's feet with onions, carrots & spices
Pieds de Mouton: mutton knuckles
Pieds de Mouton Poulette: sheep feet in broth, egg yolks & lemon
Pieds de Porc: pig's feet
Pieds de Porc Farcis à la Rouenniase: boned stuffed pig's feet
Pieds de Porc Ste. Ménéhould: pig's feet in butter & crumbs
Pieds de Porc Truffés: pig's feet with truffles
Pieds et Pacquets: mutton, tripe & feet in stew
Pieds et Pacquets Marseillais: sheep trotters with tripe
Pigeon à l'Etuvée en Casserole aux Petits Pois: pigeon casserole with green peas
Pigeon au Porto sur Lit de Ris de Veau: pigeon in port wine with veal sweetbreads
Pigeon aux Cèpes Frais: pigeon with fresh mushrooms
Pigeon Braisé aux Olives ou Navets: braised pigeon with olives or turnips
Pigeon Etuvée en Casserole aux Petits Pois: pigeon stuffed with little peas in casserole
Pigeon Grillé Sauce Diable: broiled pigeon with sauce of wine, shallots, vinegar & brown sauce
Pigeonneau à l'Ail: young pigeon with garlic
Pigeonneau Farci à la Périgourdine: young pigeon stuffed with truffles
Pigeonneau Grillé: young pigeon broiled or roasted on spit
Pilaff de Foies de Volaille: sautéed chicken livers with rice

Plateau

Pilaff de Volaille au Curry: chicken curry with rice
Piments: pimentos
Piments Doux: pimentos or bell peppers
Pinée: dried cod
Pineau des Charentes: liqueur or fresh grape juice & cognac
Pintade: Guinea fowl
Pintade à la Canadienne: Guinea hen with apples & blood sausage
Pintadeau: Guinea hen
Pintadeau à la Choucroute: Guinea hen with sauerkraut
Pintadeau au Vinaigre de Framboises: young Guinea hen with raspberry vinegar
Pintadeau en Robe d'Or: roast young Guinea hen
Pintadeau Entier Rôti: whole roasted Guinea hen
Pintadeau Farci au Romarin: Guinea hen with rosemary stuffing
Pintadeau Farci aux Pieds de Cochon: Guinea hen stuffed with pig's feet
Pintadeau Normande: Guinea hen with rich egg, cream butter & wine sauce
Pintadeau sur Canapé Flambé à l'Armagnac: flaming Guinea hen with cognac on toasted bread with intestines
Pintadeau Truffé: Guinea hen with truffles
Pintade aux Choux: Guinea hen with cabbage
Pintade Sautée Chasseur: Guinea hen sautéed with shallots, mushrooms, wine & tomatoes
Piperade: scrambled eggs with onions, Bayonne ham, sweet peppers & tomatoes
Piquante: shallots & white wine in brown sauce
Pissaladière: anchovy, onion, tomato & olive tart
Pissenlits au Lard: dandelions with bacon bits & vinegar dressing
Pistou: vegetable soup with basil & garlic
Pithiviers: cake made of puff pastry with almonds & rum or lark & liver pâté with game jelly
Pizza: pizza
Plat de Cote Gros Sel: short ribs with sour pickles & mustard
Plat de Côtes: short ribs
Plat du Jour: dish of the day
Plateau de Canapés (Saumon, Caviar, Foie Gras): tray of canapés (smoked salmon, caviar & goose liver pâté)
Plateau de Fromages: cheese tray
Plateau de Fruits de Mer: tray of assorted seafood
Plateau de Petits Fours Frais: tray of fresh petit fours

Plateau

Plateau de Petits Fours Secs: tray of dry petit fours
Plat Garni au Choix: your choice of garnished dishes
Plats de Viande, Volaille et Gibier: meat, poultry & game dishes
Plats d'Oeufs: egg dishes
Plats Mijotés: stews
Plombrières: vanilla ice cream in parfait mould with apricot jam
Plum Cake: fruit filled cake
Poché: poached
Poêlé: pan fried
Pointe de Filet: pork chop
Pointes d'Asperges: asparagus tips
Poireaux: leeks
Poireaux à la Niçoise: leeks in garlic sauce
Poireaux, aux: with leeks
Poireaux Vinaigrette: leeks with vinaigrette dressing
Poire Belle Hélène: pears with ice cream & chocolate sauce
Poire d'Avocat Calypso ou Floride: avocado pear, Florida or Calypso type
Poirée: spinach beet or chard
Poire Pochée Alma: poached pear in red wine with whipped cream
Poire Pochée en Surprise: poached pears in liqueur sauce
Poires: pears
Poires à la Dauphine: pears in vanilla syrup in puff pastry with candied fruits
Poires au Vin: pears in red wine or port
Poires Bordaloue: pastry tart with almond custard, Kirsch, red currants or apricot jam with macaroons & pears
Poires Cardinal: pears in vanilla syrup with cream & raspberry syrup
Poires Condé: pear in vanilla syrup on sweet rice with candied fruit
Poires Flambées à l'Alcool de Poire: pears flamed with pear brandy
Poires Melba: vanilla ice cream with pears in cassis sauce (black currants) or raspberries
Poires Pochées au Champagne: pears poached in Champagne
Pois Cassés: split peas
Pois Chiches: chick peas
Poisson aux Herbes du Maquis: fish with herbs
Poisson Beurre Blanc: fish with whipped butter, vinegar &

Pommes

shallots sauce
Poisson de Loire au Beurre Blanc: fish from the Loire River with butter, white wine & shallot sauce
Poissons: fish
Poissons au Beurre Blanc: fish with whipped butter, vinegar & shallot sauce
Poissons Braisés au Chablis: fish braised in white wine
Poissons Crus: raw fish
Poissons et Crustacés: fish & crustaceans
Poissons Fumés Assortis: assorted smoked fish
Poissons Grillés: broiled fish
Poitrine: breast
Poitrine d'Agneau Farcie aux Raisins: lamb breast stuffed with grapes
Poitrine de Mouton à la Ste. Ménéhould: lamb breast with bacon, onions, bay leaves & herbs
Poitrine de Mouton en Carbonnade: braised breast of lamb with garlic, ham, carrots, onions & tomato sauce
Poitrine de Veau: veal breast
Poitrine de Veau à l'Alsacienne: breast of veal with sauerkraut & goose liver
Poitrine de Veau Farcie: stuffed breast of veal
Poitrine d'Oie Fumée: smoked goose breast
Poitrine Fumée: smoked bacon
Poivrade: game stock in brown sauce
Poivre: pepper
Poivre, au: with peppercorns
Poivre Sauce: game stock, cream & peppercorns
Pojarsky de Caneton "au Vieux Bordeaux": duckling with old Bordeaux wine
Pomme: apple
Pomme de Terre: potato
Pommes à la Bordelaise: potatoes in butter with garlic
Pommes à l'Anglaise: boiled potatoes
Pommes Allumettes: French fried potatoes
Pommes au Four: baked apples
Pommes Chips: fried potato chips
Pommes de Terre: potatoes
Pommes de Terre à l'Anglaise: boiled potatoes
Pommes de Terre à la Vapeur: steamed potatoes
Pommes de Terre à l'Huile de Noix: potatoes sautéed in walnut oil
Pommes de Terre Aligot: whipped potatoes with Cantal

Pommes

cheese
Pommes de Terre Allumettes: deep fried matchstick potatoes
Pommes de Terre au Beurre: potatoes sautéed in butter
Pommes de Terre au Four: baked potatoes
Pommes de Terre Boulangère: potatoes cooked with roast
Pommes de Terre Chips: potato chips
Pommes de Terre Cocotte au Beurre: potatoes in casserole with butter
Pommes de Terre Dauphinoise: baked potatoes with garlic & cream
Pommes de Terre Duchesse: potatoes puréed with eggs
Pommes de Terre Frites: fried potatoes
Pommes de Terre Gaufrettes: waffle potatoes
Pommes de Terre Gratin Dauphinois: sliced potatoes with layers of cheese & cream
Pommes de Terre Gratin Savoyard: thin sliced potatoes with butter, cheese & broth
Pommes de Terre Mignonette: matchstick potatoes
Pommes de Terre Paillasson: deep fried straw potatoes
Pommes de Terre Sautées: potato slices sautéed in butter
Pommes de Terre Soufflées: mashed potatoes with eggs & cream
Pommes Duchesse: mashed potatoes with butter & egg yolks
Pommes Frites: French fried potatoes
Pommes Lyonnaise: potatoes with white wine, wine vinegar, onions & parsley
Pommes Mousseline: potatoes whipped with cream or mashed potatoes
Pommes Parisienne: fried potato balls
Pommes Pont Neuf: deep fried potato slices or new potatoes
Pommes Sarladaise: sliced potatoes in butter & truffles
Pommes Sautées: sautéed potatoes
Pommes Soufflées: potatoes whipped with egg & cream
Pommes Vapeur: steamed potatoes
Pompano en Papillote: pompano (fish) in parchment paper
Pontigaud: cow's milk cheese similar to Roquefort
Pont l'Evêque: Normandy cheese
Poragnère Coumtadino: pork tenderloin stuffed with braised lamb
Poragneu Coumtadino (Porc Farci de Truffes et Gigot d'Agneau): pork stuffed with truffles & lamb
Porc: pork

Poularde

Porc à la Basquaise: pork loin roasted with milk
Portion de Fromages (au Choix): selection of cheeses
Porto: brown sauce with port wine
Port Salut: creamy cheese
Portugaise: sauce of tomatoes & garlic
Portugaises: oysters
Potage à la Crème: cream soup
Potage à la Reine: chicken broth with egg custards
Potage Bonne Femme: vegetable soup
Potage Crécy: carrot soup
Potage Crème: cream soup
Potage de Champignons: mushroom soup
Potage de Légumes: vegetable soup
Potage de Tortue: turtle soup
Potage du Chef: chef's soup
Potage du Jour: soup of the day
Potage Froid: cold soup
Potage Parmentier: potato & leek soup
Potage St. Germain: pea soup
Pot au Feu: boiled beef & vegetables
Pot au Feu en Vessie: loin of pork in pig's bladder
Pot de Caviar Béluga: Beluga caviar (Persian)
Pot de Crème au Chocolat: chocolate pudding
Pot de Thé avec Lait ou Citron: pot of tea with milk or lemon
Potée: stew
Potée Auvergnate: stewed salt pork & sausages with cabbage, carrots, onions & garlic
Potée aux Haricots Rouges: stew with sausages, ham, red beans & red wine
Potée Comtoise: pork, sausage, beef, mutton & vegetable stew on bread
Potée d'Escargots: snail stew with herbs & vegetables
Potée des Pêcheurs: fish stew in earthenware pot
Potée Lorraine: vegetable stew with pork
Potiron: pumpkin
Pouding au Pain: bread pudding
Pouding au Riz: rice pudding
Pouilly Fuissé: white burgundy
Poularde à la Broche: chicken barbecued on spit
Poularde à la Crème: chicken in cream sauce
Poularde à la Crème au Champagne: roast chicken in champagne cream sauce
Poularde à la Crème d'Estragon: creamed chicken with tarragon

Poularde

Poularde à la Ficelle: tied roast chicken in broth
Poularde à la Flamande: fried chicken with mashed potatoes, braised lettuce & glazed onions
Poularde à l'Estragon: roast chicken with tarragon
Poularde Anne d'Urfe: roast chicken
Poularde au Beurre d'Ecrevisses: roast chicken stuffed with ham, liver, gizzards & herbs with lobster butter
Poularde au Citron: roast chicken with lemon
Poularde au Porto: roast chicken in port wine
Poularde au Riesling et aux Morilles: chicken with white wine & mushrooms
Poularde au Roquefort: chicken roasted with Roquefort cheese
Poularde au Vin Jaune et aux Morilles: baked chicken with wine, mushroom, cream & egg yolk sauce
Poularde aux Ecrevisses: chicken with crayfish (lobster)
Poularde aux Morilles à la Crème: chicken with cream & mushroom sauce
Poularde aux Truffes: roast chicken stuffed with truffles & butter sauce
Poularde Braisée Crème Estragon: chicken braised with cream & tarragon
Poularde de Bresse au Crécy: chicken from Bresse
Poularde de Bresse au Pot: chicken from Bresse in pot
Poularde de Bresse aux Morilles: Bresse chicken with mushrooms
Poularde de Bresse Braisée aux 2 Vinaigres: Bresse chicken braised in 2 types of vinegar
Poularde de Bresse en Brioche: Bresse chicken in pastry
Poularde de Bresse en Vessie: Bresse chicken in bladder
Poularde en Chemise: stuffed chicken in pig's intestine in broth
Poularde en Civet au Vieux Bourgogne: stewed breast of chicken with onions, bacon, mushrooms & wine
Poularde en Feuilletée: roast chicken in puff pastry
Poularde en Vessie: chicken stuffed with liver, heart, gizzard & pistachio nuts in bladder with veal & chicken broth
Poularde Flambée Ile de France: roast chicken flamed with cognac in cream, egg, broth & cognac sauce
Poularde Grillée: broiled chicken
Poularde Grillée Paillasson: chicken grilled over straw
Poularde Maxims: braised chicken with mushrooms flamed in cognac & cream sauce
Poularde Médicis: chicken with artichoke bottoms stuffed

Poulet

with peas, carrots & turnips or small potatoes or chicken with Béarnaise sauce (red wine, butter & meat juices) with tomato purée
Poularde Poêlée au Champagne aux Morilles: roast chicken with champagne & mushrooms
Poularde Sautée au Vinaigre de Xérès: old fashioned chicken in Xérès vinegar
Poularde Sautées Fines Herbes et Estragon: chicken sautéed with finely chopped herbs & tarragon
Poularde Suédoise sur Commande: Swedish chicken on special order
Poule au Pot: hen stewed with sausage & vegetables
Poule au Pot Henri IV: stuffed hen with ham, herbs, eggs, liver & garlic in broth with wine or cream sauce
Poulet: chicken
Poulet à la Basquaise: chicken with ham & mushrooms
Poulet à la Bonne Femme: chicken in butter with bacon, onions & potatoes
Poulet a la Champenoise: chicken stuffed with forcemeat & champagne
Poulet à la Crème: chicken with cream sauce
Poulet à la Milanaise: roast chicken with macaroni & tomato sauce
Poulet à la Nantaise: chicken stuffed with chestnuts, onions & parsley
Poulet à l'Anglaise: chicken with parsley sauce & potatoes
Poulet à la Niçoise: chicken in olive oil with wine, garlic, onion, tomato & black olive sauce
Poulet à l'Armenonville: chicken with artichoke hearts, tomatoes, beans & potatoes in butter
Poulet à l'Espagnole: chicken with saffron rice, artichokes, tomatoes, garlic & pimentos
Poulet à l'Estragon: chicken with tarragon
Poulet au Bourgogne: chicken in Burgundy wine
Poulet au Champagne: chicken in champagne
Poulet au Fromage: chicken with cheese
Poulet au Paprika: paprika chicken
Poulet au Pot Farcie: stuffed chicken with crumbs, eggs, herbs & broth
Poulet au Vinaigre: chicken in vinegar
Poulet aux Ecrevisses: chicken with crayfish (lobster)
Poulet aux Morilles: chicken with mushrooms
Poulet aux Morilles à la Crème: chicken with creamed mushrooms

Poulet

Poulet aux Nouilles: chicken with noodles
Poulet aux Pignons: chicken with pine nuts
Poulet Basquaise: chicken with peppers, onions & rice
Poulet Bouilli: boiled chicken
Poulet Bresse au Vinaigre: Bresse chicken in vinegar
Poulet Cocotte: chicken with pork & ham slices
Poulet Comtoise: sautéed chicken with white wine & broth
Poulet Coq au Vin: young cock chicken stewed in red wine
Poulet de Bresse à la Crème: roast Bresse chicken in cream sauce
Poulet de Bresse à la Crème aux Morilles: Bresse chicken with creamed mushrooms
Poulet de Bresse à l'Estragon: chicken from Bresse with tarragon
Poulet de Bresse au Champagne: Bresse chicken with champagne
Poulet de Bresse au Feu de Bois: spit roasted Bresse chicken
Poulet de Bresse au Vinaigre: Bresse chicken with vinegar
Poulet de Bresse Grillé Sauce Diable, Pommes Vapeur: braised Bresse chicken with hot sauce & boiled potatoes
Poulet de Bresse Rôti: roast Bresse chicken
Poulet de Bresse Sauté à l'Estragon: Bresse chicken with tarragon
Poulet de Grain à la Vézulienne: spring chicken stuffed with salt pork & liver in pie crust with butter sauce
Poulet de Grain à l'Estragon: young chicken with tarragon, broth, egg yolk & cream sauce
Poulet de Grain aux Morilles: spring chicken with mushrooms
Poulet de Grain Rôti aux Aromates et Pouilly: spring chicken roasted with aromatic spices & white wine
Poulet de Grain Sauté au Vin de Jérez: spring chicken sautéed in wine (sherry)
Poulet des Gastronomes: duck liver stuffed in chicken with mushrooms & port wine sauce
Poulet Docteur: braised chicken with truffles & cream
Poulet en Meurette: chicken in red wine with salt pork, onions, garlic & mushrooms
Poulet "Fermier Normandie": chicken in casserole with vegetables & cider with cream
Poulet Flambé au Calvados: chicken flamed with Calvados wine
Poulet Fourré à l'Oseille: roast chicken stuffed with sorrel

Poussin

(lettuce like herb)
Poulet Fricassé: stewed chicken
Poulet Frites: chicken & French fries
Poulet Froid en Gelée à l'Estragon: cold chicken in tarragon flavored aspic
Poulet Froid Mayonnaise: cold chicken with mayonnaise
Poulet Grillé à la Broche, Sauce Selon Désir: chicken broiled on spit with choice of sauces
Poulet Grillé à la Diable: chicken broiled with white wine, shallots & herbs
Poulet Grillé Sauce Diable: broiled chicken with hot & spicy sauce of shallots, white wine, wine vinegar, meat juice gravy & finely chopped herbs
Poulet Henri IV: stuffed poached chicken
Poulet Mère Michel: flamed chicken stuffed with tarragon & topped with sauce of pan juices & cream
Poulet Ouvert et Sauté au Vin Blanc: chicken sautéed in white wine
Poulet Paul Gauguin: sautéed chicken with baked banana & blood sausage
Poulet Poché: chicken with rice & cream sauce
Poulet Rôti: roast chicken
Poulet Rôti Garni: roast chicken with herbs
Poulet Sauté: pan fried chicken
Poulet Sauté à l'Ail: chicken sautéed with garlic
Poulet Sauté à l'Estragon: tarragon chicken sautéed with fried onions & potatoes
Poulet Sauté au Champagne: chicken sautéed in champagne
Poulet Sauté au Pouilly: sautéed chicken in white wine
Poulet Sauté aux Cèpes: chicken sautéed with mushrooms
Poulet Sauté aux Ecrevisses: sautéed chicken with crayfish (lobster)
Poulet Sauté aux Tomates: chicken sautéed with tomatoes
Poulet Sauté Bordelaise: chicken sautéed in olive oil with bacon, onions, garlic & artichoke bottoms
Poulette Sauce: chicken stock with egg yolks & cream
Poulet Vallée d'Auge: sautéed chicken with cider, cream, egg yolks & sautéed apples
Poulpe: small octopus
Poulpe au Riz: octopus with rice
Pounti: vegetable pie
Poussin: roasted young chicken
Poussin au Miel Fondu Flambé au Cognac: young chicken in

Poussin
honey flaming with cognac
Poussin aux Morilles: young chicken with mushrooms
Poussin Dauphinois aux Morilles à la Crème: sautéed young chicken with mushrooms in cream sauce of white wine & egg yolks
Poussin en Surprise: boned stuffed young chicken with wine sauce
Poussin Grillé Moutarde: young roasted chicken with mustard sauce
Poussin Poêlé Périgourdine: fresh young chicken in truffle sauce
Praire: clam with a round thick shell eaten raw or baked
Prawn: large shrimp
Prawn Cocktail: large shrimp with dressing of mayonnaise, tomato catsup & herbs
Pré Salé: lamb which has grazed on meadows near the sea washed with salt water
Pression, à la: on tap (beer)
Presskopf: slices of head cheese
Primeurs: tiny young vegetables
Prix Fixe: fixed price menu for complete meals
Produits de la Mer: seafood
Profiteroles au Café: small cream puffs with whipped cream or ice cream & covered with coffee flavored sauce
Profiteroles au Chocolat: small cream puffs with whipped cream or ice cream with chocolate sauce
Profiteroles de Cervelle: cream puff pastry balls with calf's brains & sauce
Profiteroles Glacées au Chocolat: cream puffs iced or glazed with chocolate
Provençale: sauce of beans, pork, goose with garlic & crumbs or tomato sauce with garlic & basil
Provençales: scallops with white wine, garlic & olive oil
Prune: plum
Pruneau: prune
Pruneaux en Chemise: prunes in cooking parchment
Prunes Flambées: cooked plums flamed with plum brandy or Mirabelle
Pudding Glacé: frozen pudding
Punch Glacé: iced punch
Purée de Palombe à la Bazadaise: pigeon purée with minced veal, truffles & liver
Purée de Foie: liver purée in butter
Purées de Gibier: game soups

Queues

Purées de Légumes: vegetable soups
Purées de Volaille: poultry soups
Quart: cow's milk cheese or quarter of
Quartier d'Agneau Persillé Pommes Nouvelles: rack of lamb with parsley & new potatoes
Quasi: veal from the rump end of the loin
Quatre Quarts: cake mixed with candied fruit, almonds & raisins
Quatre Saisons: cake with butter cream & almonds
Quenelle au Gratin: dumpling with grated cheese & bread crumbs
Quenelle Châtelaine: dumplings with chicken or meat & chestnuts in broth
Quenelle de Brochet Brillat Savarin: pike dumplings with scalloped potatoes, pâté, truffles & asparagus tips
Quenelle Financière: dumplings with giblets, sweetbreads, mushrooms & truffles
Quenelles: dumpling of meat, chicken or fish with bread crumbs, fat & eggs
Quenelles à la Crème: cream dumplings
Quenelles Atlantique: dumplings with seafood
Quenelles de Brochet: pike dumplings
Quenelles de Brochet à la Crème: creamed pike dumplings
Quenelles de Brochet au Pernod et l'Estragon: pike dumplings with Pernod (licorice flavored liqueur) & tarragon
Quenelles de Brochet aux Ecrevisses: pike dumplings with crayfish (lobster)
Quenelles de Brochet du Lac: lake pike dumplings
Quenelles de Brochet Mazarin: pike dumplings with tartlets, truffles & shrimp sauce
Quenelles de Brochet Nantua: pike dumplings with Nantua sauce (cream, fish stock, vegetables, crayfish (lobster) sauce)
Quenelles de Volaille: dumplings with chicken breast in cream, eggs & nutmeg
Quetsch Fourées: stuffed prunes
Queue: tail
Queue de Boeuf: oxtail
Queue de Boeuf à la Ste. Ménéhould: poached oxtail in crumbs
Queue de Boeuf Farcie: stuffed oxtail sautéed with vegetables
Queue de Veau: calf's tail
Queues d'Ecrevisses à la Vinaigrette: crayfish tails (lobster)

Queues

marinated in vinaigrette dressing
Queues de Langoustes au Beurre à l'Ail: lobster tails in garlic butter
Quiche de Homard: eggs & cream in pastry with lobster
Quiche Lorraine: eggs, cream & bacon in crust
Râble de Lièvre: saddle of rabbit
Râble de Lièvre (Saison de Chasse): saddle of rabbit during the hunting season only
Râble de Lièvre Dijonnaise: saddle of hare in Dijon mustard, white wine & cream
Râble de Lièvre Sauce Poivrade: saddle of hare with red wine & pepper gravy with gooseberry jelly & chestnut purée
Raclette: chunk of melting cheese with potatoes, pickles & onions
Raclette à l'Aisienne: melted cheese with boiled potatoes
Radish: radishes with butter & salt
Radis Beurre-Andouille: radishes with butter & smoked sausage
Ragoût: stew
Ragoût d'Ecrevisses au Sauterne: stewed crayfish (lobster) with white wine
Ragoût de Fruits de Mer (En Saison): stew of seafood in season
Ragoût de Homard aux Truffes: lobster stew with truffles
Ragout de Mouton: breast of lamb with vegetables & white wine
Ragoût de Queues d'Ecrevisses: crayfish (lobster) tail stew
Ragoût de Queues d'Ecrevisses Sauce Nage: crayfish (lobster) tail stew with fish & vegetable broth
Ragoût de Ris de Veau: veal sweetbread stew
Ragoût d'Escargots aux Cèpes: stewed snails & mushrooms
Ragoût de Truffes: stew of meats or vegetables with truffles
Ragoût de Veau: veal stew
Ragoût Fin du Pot au Feu: beef stew
Raie: skate or ray (fish)
Raie au Beurre Noir: poached ray (fish) with brown butter
Raie au Beurre Noisette: poached ray (fish) in brown butter with lemon juice
Raie aux Câpres: ray (fish) with capers
Raie Grenobloise: poached ray (fish) with vinegar, browned butter, capers & parsley
Raie Sauce Moutarde: ray (fish) with mustard
Raifort: horseradish
Raisins: grapes

Ris

Ramequin a là Neuchâteloise: small cheese tart
Ramequin de Moules: small casseroles of baked mussels with cheese
Rascasse: bony fish
Ratatouille: stew with tomatoes, eggplant, onions, sweet peppers, zucchini, garlic & olive oil
Ravigote: vinaigrette sauce with capers
Ravioles Gratin: ravioli with cheese & bread crumbs
Ravioles Locales: local style ravioli
Raviolis Piémontaise: ravioli with rice & truffles
Reblochon: semi-hard cow's milk cheese
Religieuse: dessert of 3 éclairs with butter cream
Remoulade: mayonnaise with mustard, pickles, eggs & capers
Rillettes: pork cooked in its own fat made into pâté
Rillettes de la Sarthe: cooked pork, goose or rabbit in pastry crust
Rillettes de Porc: soft potted pork
Rillettes d'Oie: goose cooked in lard
Rillons: pork cooked in pork fat or pork & pork lard in crock
Ris: sweetbreads
Ris d'Agneau: lamb sweetbreads
Ris de Veau: veal sweetbreads
Ris de Veau à la Lyonnaise: calf's sweetbreads sautéed with onions, parsley, garlic & tarragon
Ris de Veau à la Normande: veal sweetbreads with cider
Ris de Veau à la Parme: veal sweetbreads with ham
Ris de Veau à l'Orange: veal sweetbreads sautéed with orange sauce
Ris de Veau au Citron: veal sweetbreads with lemon
Ris de Veau aux Ecrevisses: veal sweetbreads with crayfish (lobster)
Ris de Veau aux Morilles: veal sweetbreads with mushrooms
Ris de Veau aux Queues d'Ecrevisses: veal sweetbreads with crayfish (lobster) tails
Ris de Veau Braisé: braised veal sweetbreads
Ris de Veau Braisé Sauce Périgueux: braised sweetbreads with truffle sauce
Ris de Veau Dauphinoise: veal sweetbreads with Gruyère cheese (like Swiss) in milk
Ris de Veau en Cocotte: veal sweetbreads in flameproof dish
Ris de Veau Farci aux Ecrevisses: veal sweetbreads with crayfish (lobster)
Ris de Veau Gastronome: gastronomical veal sweetbreads

Ris

Ris de Veau Lorraine: sweetbreads braised with bacon, garlic, mushrooms & white wine

Ris de Veau Maréchal: veal sweetbreads with chicken dumplings, truffles, cockscombs & sherry

Ris de Veau Normande: veal sweetbreads sautéed in heavy cream sauce with sautéed apples in cider

Ris de Veau Papillote: veal sweetbreads in oiled parchment paper

Ris de Veau Périgourdine: veal sweetbreads with truffles

Ris de Veau Princesse: veal sweetbreads with artichoke bottoms with asparagus tips, potatoes & cream sauce

Ris de Veau Talleyrand: veal sweetbreads with sauce of vegetables, truffles, sherry, pickled tongue & cream

Ris de Veau Toulousaine: veal sweetbreads with chicken dumplings, cockscombs, mushrooms, truffles & sauce Allemande (blond cream sauce)

Ris de Veau Véronique: veal sweetbreads with grape sauce

Rissoles: puff pastries with meat or fish

Rissoles de Poisson: puff pastry with fish

Rissoles de Truffes: deep fried pastry puff with truffles

Riz: rice

Riz au Caramel: rice pudding with caramel

Riz Condé: rice pudding with milk, sugar, whipped cream & strawberries

Riz Condé Amandine: rice pudding with milk, sugar eggs, vanilla, roasted almonds & whipped cream

Riz Condé aux Fruits: rice pudding with fruit slices & apricot glaze

Riz Pilaf à la Valencienne: rice stewed with vegetables

Rizotto Pêcheur: rice with various fish & seafood with grated cheese

Robert: mustardy tomato brown sauce in wine

Rocher de Glace: 4 flavors of ice cream in mold

Rognon Châteaubriand: kidneys in wine & herb-lemon sauce

Rognon de Veau à la Moutarde: veal kidneys with mustard

Rognon de Veau au Chablis: veal kidneys in Chablis (wine)

Rognon de Veau Flambé au Calvados: veal kidneys flamed with Calvados cider

Rognon de Veau Moutartier Flambé Grande Fine: flaming veal kidneys with cognac & mustard

Rognon de Veau Principauté: veal kidneys of the principality

Rogonnade: cut of veal with the kidneys in it

Rognons: kidneys or kidney shaped cream puffs iced like éclairs

Rognons

Rognons au Baies de Genievre: veal kidneys with juniper berries & gin in brown sauce
Rognons aux Cèpes: veal kidneys sautéed with mushrooms, shallots & brown sauce
Rognons Berrichonne: veal kidneys sautéed in meat & wine sauce with mushrooms & bacon
Rognons Coq Hardi: kidneys
Rognons d'Agneau: lamb kidneys
Rognons d'Agneau au Roquefort: lamb kidneys with Roquefort cheese sauce
Rognons de Boeuf: beef kidneys
Rognons de Boeuf à la Parisienne: beef kidneys seasoned & sautéed
Rognons de Mouton: mutton kidneys
Rognons de Veau: veal kidneys
Rognons de Veau a la Bordelaise: sautéed veal kidneys with onions, garlic, red wine & mushrooms in brown sauce
Rognons de Veau au Chablis: veal kidneys roasted with wine sauce
Rognons de Veau au Genièvre: veal kidneys with juniper berries or gin
Rognons de Veau au Marsala: veal kidneys in wine
Rognons de Veau au Vinaigre: veal kidneys in vinegar
Rognons de Veau aux Apserges: veal kidneys with asparagus
Rognons de Veau aux Echalottes: veal kidneys with shallots
Rognons de Veau Berrichonne: veal kidneys sautéed in butter with salt pork & onions, mushrooms & red wine or veal kidneys with glazed onions, chestnuts, bacon & cabbage
Rognons de Veau Dijonnaise: veal kidneys with mustard
Rognons de Veau en Brochette, Vert Pré: veal kidneys on skewers with watercress & French fries
Rognons de Veau Escoffier: veal kidneys with sauce
Rognons de Veau Flambés: veal kidneys flamed in cognac with cream & wine sauce
Rognons de Veau Flambés aux Champignons: flaming veal kidneys with mushrooms
Rognons de Veau Flambés Lasserre: flaming veal kidneys in pastry casserole
Rognons de Veau Grillés: broiled veal kidneys
Rognons de Veau Jardinière: veal kidneys with vegetables
Rognons de Veau Madère: veal kidneys with Madeira wine
Rognons de Veau Sautés: sautéed veal kidneys
Rognons de Veau Sautés Morvandelle: veal kidneys sautéed

Rognons

with ham, tomatoes & mushrooms
Rognons Flambés: veal kidneys flamed in brandy with wine sauce with mushrooms
Rognons Grillés Béarnaise: broiled kidneys in Béarnaise sauce (red wine, seasonings, butter & egg yolks)
Rognons Montpensier: sautéed veal kidneys in Madeira wine sauce with asparagus, artichoke bottoms, truffles & potato balls
Rognons Vert Pré: veal kidneys on skewer with watercress, potatoes, parsley & lemon butter
Rollmops: pickled fillets of herring around piece of onion & pickles
Romarin: rosemary (herb)
Romsteck: rib steak
Rosette: sausage made from the shoulder meat of pork
Rosette d'Agneau Camarguaise: boned lamb cutlets with garlic & tomato
Rosette de Lyon: thinly sliced sausage
Rosette de Savoie: rose shaped sponge cake of wheat & potato flour
Rosettes de Homard Hawaïïenne: lobster with fresh pineapple
Rôti de Boeuf au Jus: roast beef in its own juices
Rôti de Boeuf Jardiniere: roast beef with vegetables
Rôti de Caneton: roast duckling
Rôti de Porc aux Marrons: roast pork with chestnuts in brown sauce
Rôti de Porc aux Mirabelles: roast pork with plums
Rôti de Poulet Nouveau: roast spring chicken
Rôtie: slice of toasted or baked bread
Rouelle de Jarret de Boeuf Braisé: braised beef knuckle
Rouelle de Veau: slices of veal knuckle in white wine
Rouennais à la Rouennaise: Rouen duck with red wine & duck liver sauce
Rouget: fish like red mullet
Rouget en Papillote: red mullet in parchment paper
Rouget Grillé Beurre d'Anchois: tiny red mullet with anchovy butter
Rougets à l'Orientale: red mullets in white wine, shallots, thyme, bay leaves, celery, fennel (licorice flavored herb), peppercorns & saffron
Rougets au Four Mirabeau: baked red mullets with anchovy filets, olives, tarragon & anchovy butter
Rougets Grillés: broiled red mullet

Salade

Rouget Soufflé: red mullet soufflé
Rouille: sauce usually for bouillabaisse (fish soup) with peppers, crumbs & oil or hot peppers & mayonnaise sauce
Roulade de Filets de Sole: rolled filets of sole usually stuffed
Roulades de Poisson: fish rolls
Roulage Chocolat: chocolate roll with whipped cream in powdered sugar
Roulage Confiture: jelly roll
Roquefort: strong blue cheese
Russe: mayonnaise with caviar & mustard
Sabayon (Zabaglione): custard of egg yolk & wine
Sabayon au Grand Marnier: egg custard made with orange liqueur
Sabayon à Votre Choix: your choice of wine custard
Sabayon Froid aux Avelines: wine custard with hazelnuts
Sablé: biscuit or cookie with jam or cream mixture
Saignant: rare (meat)
Sainte Maure: soft goat's milk cheese
Saint Honoré: cake with cream puffs & whipped cream
Saint Jacques Mornay: scallops with creamy cheese sauce
Saint Nectaire: semi-hard cheese
Saint Paulin: semi-hard cheese
Saint Pierre Carcopino Farci à l'Oseille: fish stuffed with sorrel (lettuce like herb)
Saint Pierre Maison: fish in the style of the house
Saison de Chasse: available only in the hunting season
Salade à l'Allemande: salad of potatoes & apples with beetroot, onions & mayonnaise with gherkin & salt herring
Salade à l'Huile de Noix: salad with walnut oil
Salade Angèlina: mixed salad with chicken, ham, Gruyere cheese & French dressing
Salade au Chapon: bread rubbed with garlic & sprinkled with olive oil & served with salads
Salade Auvergnate: cabbage salad
Salade de Carotte Rapée: grated carrot salad
Salade de Betteraves: picked beet salad
Salade de Cervelas: sausage salad
Salade de Caviar: caviar salad with onions, peppers, lemon & mayonnaise
Salade de Chou-Fleur: cauliflower salad
Salade de Concombres: cucumber salad
Salade de Crabes d'URSS: Russian crab salad
Salade de Crevettes: shrimp salad
Salade de Fonds d'Artichauts et Pointes d'Asperges: salad

Salade

of artichoke bottoms & asparagus tips
Salade de Fruits: fruit salad
Salade de Fruits aux Liqueurs: fruit salad in liqueurs
Salade de Fruits Rafraîchis: salad of fruits in liqueur
Salade de Gruyère: cheese salad
Salade de Homard: lobster salad
Salade de Homard aux Truffes: lobster salad with truffles
Salade de Laitue: lettuce salad
Salade de Langouste: crayfish (lobster) salad with mayonnaise & greens
Salad de Maïs: salad with corn
Salade Demi-Deuil: potatoes & truffle salad with cream & mustard
Salade d'Endives: endive salad
Salade de Pêcheurs aux Xérès: fish or seafood salad with sherry
Salade d'Epinards: spinach salad
Salade de Poisson: fish salad
Salade de Pommes: potato salad
Salade de Poulet: chicken salad
Salade de Queues de Langoustines: lobster tail salad
Salade de Saison: salad with seasonal ingredients
Salade de Thon: tuna salad
Salade de Tomates: tomato salad
Salade de Truite: trout salad
Salade d'Oeufs: egg salad
Salade du Chef: chef's salad
Salade Favorite: crayfish (lobster), asparagus & truffle salad oil & vinegar dressing
Salade Frissée aux Lardons: salad with bacon bits
Salade Laitue: salad with Boston lettuce
Salade Mâche: corn salad
Salade Maison: house salad
Salade Mesclun: young mixed greens salad
Salade Mixte: mixed green salad
Salade Nicoise: salad of cucumbers, anchovies, tomatoes, tuna, peppers & olives
Salade Panachée: mixed herb salad
Salade Pissenlits: dandelion green salad
Salade Rachel: endive, red beet & walnut salad
Salade Romaine: romaine lettuce salad
Salade Tourangelle (Lardons et Oeuf Poché): salad with bacon bits & poached egg pieces
Salades au Lard: greens with bacon bits, bacon fat & bread

Sauce

crust rubbed with garlic
Salade Scarole: escarole lettuce salad
Salades Diverses: various salads
Salade Verte: green salad
Salade Verte de Saison: green salad with vegetables in season
Saladier Lyonnais: cold mutton feet, cold roast fowl liver, hard boiled eggs & marinated herring filets with vinaigrette dressing
Salami de Cremona: beef & pork salami
Salmis: red wine brown sauce for game or any dish made with wild game
Salmis de Bécasse: roast woodcock in chafing dish
Salmis de Col Vert: roast game in chafing dish with cabbage
Salmis de Corbeaux: crow stew
Salmis d'Ecureuil: squirrel stew
Salmis de Palombes: pigeon or dove with game stock & port or sherry in chafing dish
Salmis de Palombes aux Cèpes: roast pigeon in chafing dish with mushrooms
Salmon Coulibiac: salmon with stuffing & spinach in yeast dough
Salsifis: oyster plant (parsnip like plant with oyster flavor)
Sancerre: white Loire wine
Sandre: perch like fresh water fish
Sandre de Loire Grillé Beurre Blanc: broiled Loire perch with butter, shallot & wine sauce
Sandwich Baguette: sandwich on French bread
Sandwich Jambon de Paris: sandwich with Paris ham
Sanglier: wild boar
Sanglier à l'Auvergnate: braised wild boar with pork belly, vegetables & red wine
Sansonnet: young mackerel
Sarcelle: small wild duck
Sarcelle à l'Ancienne: wild duck breast with stock & lemon
Sardines à l'Huile: sardines marinated with oil
Sardines à l'Huile, Beurre: sardines with butter
Sardines au Beurre: sardines with butter
Sar Flambé au Fenouil: flamed sea bass with fennel (licorice flavored vegetable)
Sarrasin: buckwheat
Sauce Béarnaise: wine, butter, egg yolk & herb sauce
Sauce Hollandaise: cream, egg yolks & lemon juice, pepper

Sauces

sauce
Sauces — Chaud: hot sauces
Sauces — Froid: cold sauces
Saucisse: sausage
Saucisse Sèche: dried sausage
Saucisse Sèche des Vans: dried sausage
Saucisse Sèche du Rouergue: dry sausage from Rouergue
Saucisson: large pork sausage or dry sausage (salami)
Saucisson à l'Ail: garlic sausage
Saucisson au Champagne: sausage in champagne
Saucisson Chaud: poached sausage with salad or large hot sausage
Saucisson Chaud Pommes à l'Huile: large hot sausage with potato salad
Saucisson de Foie: liver sausage
Saucisson en Brioche: small sausage in yeast cake loaf
Saucisson Sec: dry sausage (salami)
Saucisson Sous la Cendre: charcoal broiled sausage
Saumon à l'Oseille: salmon with sorrel (lettuce like herb)
Saumon au Champagne: salmon with champagne
Saumon au Gril: grilled salmon
Saumon au Riesling: salmon in white wine
Saumon Braisé: braised salmon
Saumon Chambord: salmon in butter & red wine with glazed onions, mushrooms & fish dumplings
Saumon Cru Mariné: marinated raw salmon
Saumon de la Nouvelle Ecosse: Nova Scotia salmon
Saumon de Loire Beurre Blanc: Loire River salmon with white wine & herb-butter sauce
Saumon de Loire Grillé: broiled Loire River salmon
Saumon Doria: scallops of salmon in butter
Saumon en Malelotte: salmon steamed in butter with onions, shallots, garlic & red wine
Saumon Frais à l'Oseille: fresh salmon with sorrel (lettuce like herb)
Saumon Frais au Champagne: fresh salmon with champagne
Saumon Frais Braisé à l'Oseille: fresh salmon braised with sorrel (lettuce like herb)
Saumon Frais Fumé Danois: Danish smoked salmon
Saumon Frais Grillé Sauce Béarnaise: fresh broiled salmon with Béarnaise sauce (wine, egg yolk & herb sauce)
Saumon Fumé: smoked salmon with capers & olive oil
Saumon Fumé à la Danoise: Danish smoked salmon

Selle

Saumon Fumé au Sorbet de Raifort: smoked salmon in horseradish sauce
Saumon Fumé Maison: house smoked salmon
Saumon Fumé sur Toasts: smoked salmon on toast
Saumon Grenobloise: salmon sautéed in butter
Saumon Grillé Béarnaise: broiled salmon with Béarnaise sauce (egg yolks, white wine, herbs & butter sauce)
Saumon Grillé, Sauce Béarnaise: grilled steak with Béarnaise sauce (egg yolks, white wine, herbs & butter sauce)
Saumon Grillé Sauce Tartare: broiled salmon with tartar sauce
Saumon Mariné "Ripé": marinated salmon
Saumon Poché ou Grillé: poached or grilled salmon
Saumon Soufflé au Vermouth: salmon soufflé with vermouth
Saur: salted smoked herring
Sauté: pan fried or sautéed
Sauté de Scupions a la Niçoise: sautéed squid with tomato & anchovies
Sauté de Veau: veal chunks sautéed or gently pan fried
Sauté de Veau à la Minute: sautéed boned shoulder chops of veal
Sauté de Veau a l'Estragon: veal sautéed in wine, tarragon & with rice
Savarin: light yeast dough with liqueur or brandy fruits or whipped cream
Scaloppine Affrodite: veal with bread crumbs, egg, flour, cheeses, ham, tomatoes & truffles
Scampi: large shrimp
Sampi à la Provençale: scampi in garlic butter
Scampi à l'Indienne: scampi in white wine sauce with mushrooms & curry sauce
Scampi en Brochette: skewered scampi
Scampis Frits: fried scampi
Scampis Fritti: French fried scampi
Scampis Meuniérè: floured scampi fried in lemon butter sauce
Scampis Provençale: scampi with garlic butter
Schaschlik: shish kebab
Sel: salt
Selle d'Agneau: roast saddle of lamb
Selle d'Agneau en Chevreuil Sauce Poivrade: saddle of lamb with pepper-wine sauce, chestnut purée & gooseberry jelly

Selle

Selle d'Agneau en Croûte: baked saddle of lamb in crust
Selle d'Agneau Grillée Vert Pré: saddle of lamb with fried potatoes
Selle d'Agneau Renaissance: saddle of lamb with artichoke hearts, vegetables & cauliflower with Hollandaise sauce
Selle d'Agneau Rôtie: saddle of lamb roasted with garlic
Selle d'Agneau Rôtie à la Béarnaise: roast saddle of lamb with Béarnaise sauce & browned potatoes
Selle d'Agneau Rôtie Basquaise: roast saddle of lamb with mint leaves & Béarnaise sauce
Selle de Chevreuil Grand Veneur: saddle of venison with peppery sauce, red currant jelly & cream
Selle de Mouton: saddle of mutton
Selle de Renne: saddle of reindeer
Selle de Veau à la Flamande: saddle of veal with mashed potatoes, carrots, braised lettuce & glazed onions
Selle et Carré d'Agneau Rôtis: roast saddle & rack of lamb
Sépiole: cuttlefish
Septmoncel: blue cheese from cow's milk & goat's milk
Service Compris: tip included in the menu prices
Service Non Compris: tip not included in menu prices
Smitaine: sour cream sauce for veal, game or chicken
Socca: chick peas
Soissons: white dried beans
Sole à la Crème: filet of sole in court broth & heavy cream
Sole à la Quimperoise: filet of sole in white wine with potatoes
Sole à la Richelieu: breaded sole with cream, white wine & truffles
Sole à l'Estragon: sole with tarragon or tarragon cream sauce
Sole Alexandra: poached filet of sole with lobster slices & asparagus tips
Sole à l'Oseille: sole with sorrel (lettuce like herb)
Sole Ambassade: sole with lobster with lobster sauce
Sole Américaine: sole with lobster & sauce Américaine (pounded fish, lobster & coral (eggs), with butter, brandy, white wine & cream sauce)
Sole Anglaise des Gourmtes: English sole
Sole Argenteuil: sole with white wine sauce & asparagus
Sole au Champagne: sole in champagne
Sole au Foie Gras: sole with duck or goose livers
Sole au Gratin: sole with cheese & bread crumbs topping
Sole au Nouilly: sole in wine or vermouth

Sole

Sole au Plat: filet of sole on platter
Sole au Pouilly: sole in white wine sauce
Sole au Vermouth: sole in vermouth
Sole Bagatelle: sole stuffed with lobster meat
Sole Belle Meunière: lightly floured sole fried in lemon butter
Sole Bonne Femme: sole with onions & mushrooms
Sole Bordelaise: filet of sole with Bordeaux red wine & broth with sauce Bordelaise
Sole Braisée au Vermouth: sole braised in vermouth
Sole Braisée Vin Rouge: braised sole in red wine
Sole Caprice: crumbed filet of sole with banana & capers
Sole Cardinal: filet of sole with lobster paste & cream sauce or sole filets with lobster & truffles
Sole Champagne: sole in champagne
Sole Colbert: sole in egg & bread crumbs with seasoned butter OR sole with Colbert sauce (butter, lemon juice & parsley)
Sole Dieppoise: sole with white wine sauce, shrimp, mussels & mushrooms
Sole en Goujonettes: deep fried strips of sole
Sole Etuvée: poached filet of sole
Sole Farcie: stuffed sole
Sole Farcie au Gratin: stuffed sole in white wine sauce with cheese & bread crumbs
Sole Fécampoise: sole with shrimp sauce & mussels
Sole Fines Herbes: white wine sauce over sole with parsley
Sole Florentine: sole with spinach Mornay sauce (cheesy white sauce) & grated cheese
Sole Fourrée au Fumet de Meursault: stuffed sole in wine
Sole Fourrée Newburg: sole stuffed with seafood in sherry, butter, cream & egg yolks
Sole Frite: fried sole
Sole Grillée: broiled sole
Sole Grillée Beurre Blanc: grilled sole with white butter sauce
Sole Jeannette: sole stuffed with fish paste liver pâté
Sole Marguery: filet of sole with shrimp & mussels
Sole Marinière: filet of sole with oysters & mushrooms
Sole Meunière: sole sautéed in lemon & butter
Sole Meunière aux Courgettes: Dover sole sautéed in butter with zucchini
Sole Mireille: sole fried in oil & Béarnaise sauce (white wine, butter & cream sauce)
Sole Newburg: sole with lobster Newburg (sauce of butter, cream & eggs)

Sole

Sole Normande: sole in white wine with oysters, mussels, crayfish (lobster), mushrooms, smelts, truffles & creamy egg sauce
Sole Océan: ocean sole
Sole Otéro: baked potatoes with shrimp in white wine sauce, filets of sole & sauce Mornay (cheesy white sauce)
Sole Pompadour: broiled sole in butter & bread crumbs
Sole Portugaise: sole with white wine sauce, tomatoes, onions & mushrooms
Soles de Douvres à l'Impératrice: Dover sole with foie gras, truffles, mushrooms, dumplings or sweetbreads & wine sauce
Soles de Douvres Bonne Femme: poached Dover Sole with white wine sauce, parsley, mushrooms & shallots
Soles d Douvres d'Antin: Dover sole in white wine sauce with shallots, mushrooms, truffles & parsley
Soles de Douvres en Goujon: fried strips of Dover sole
Soles de Douvres Frites ou Grillées: fried or broiled Dover sole
Soles de Douvres Meunière: Dover sole with lemon butter
Soles de Douvres Normande: braised filet of Dover sole in egg cream butter sauce with seafood & mushrooms
Soles de Douvres Véronique: baked or poached filets of Dover sole in white wine & white grapes
Soles de Douvres Walenska: filet of Dover sole in fish fumet with slices of poached lobster, truffles & sauce Mornay (cheesy white sauce)
Sole Soufflée: sole soufflé
Sole Soufflée au Corail d'Oursins: soufflé of sole with sea urchin roe (eggs)
Sole Véronique: filet of sole in fish broth & white wine & Hollandaise sauce
Sole Walenska: poached sole with lobster & truffles in Mornay sauce (cheesy white sauce)
Sommelier: wine steward
Sorbet: sherbet
Sorbet à l'Ananas: pineapple sherbet
Sorbet à la Mandarine: tangerine sherbet
Sorbet à la Poire Williams: pear brandy sherbet
Sorbet à l'Armagnac: brandy sherbet
Sorbet à l'Orange: orange sherbet
Sorbet au Cassis: black currant sherbet
Sorbet au Choix: your choice of sherbet
Sorbet au Citron: lemon sherbet

Soufflé

Sorbet aux Fraises: strawberry sherbet
Sorbet aux Framboises: raspberry sherbet
Sorbet aux Fruits Frais: fresh fruit sherbet
Sorbet aux Poires: pear sherbet
Sorbet avec Liqueur/Petits Fours: sherbet with liqueur & petits fours (small puffs)
Sorbet de Fruits: fruit sherbet
Sorbet Poire Williams: pear brandy sherbet
Sorrel: lettuce like herb
Soubise: white sauce with purée of onions in butter
Soufflé: milk, eggs, flour base with egg whites & fish, fowl, meat or fruit purée
Soufflé à la Chartreuse: vanilla cream soufflé with Chartreuse liqueur
Soufflé à la Maltaise: cream soufflé, Curaçao liqueur & juice of blood oranges
Soufflé à la Poire: pear soufflé
Soufflé à la Vanilla: vanilla flavored soufflé
Soufflé à l'Orange: soufflé with Grand Marnier liqueur
Soufflé Ambassadrice: vanilla cream soufflé with macaroons in rum & almonds
Soufflé Andrain: Grand Marnier liqueur soufflé
Soufflé au Chocolat: chocolate flavored soufflé
Soufflé au Citron: lemon flavored soufflé
Soufflé au Grand Marnier: orange liqueur soufflé
Soufflé au Moka: soufflé with coffee flavor & cognac
Soufflé au Praline de Noisettes: toasted sugared hazelnut soufflé
Soufflé aux Fraises: soufflé with strawberries
Soufflé aux Framboises: meringue soufflé with raspberries & raspberry brandy
Soufflé aux Noisettes: toasted hazelnut soufflé
Soufflé Chaud "Gerbe de Blé": hot wheat germ soufflé
Soufflé Créole: soufflé of tomatoes, onions, celery, green peppers, hot spices & herbs
Soufflé de Barbue: bream (fish) soufflé
Soufflé de Brochet à la Bisque d'Ecrevisses: pike soufflé with creamed crayfish (lobster) soup
Soufflé de Brochet à l'Oseille: pike soufflé with sorrel (lettuce like herb)
Soufflé de Brochet Ermitage: pike soufflé with white wine
Soufflé d'Ecrevisses: soufflé with crayfish (lobster) tails
Soufflé d'Ecrevisses à la Lyonnaise: crayfish (lobster) soufflé

Soufflé

with onions in white wine
Soufflé de Féra à l'Oseille: salmon-trout soufflé with sorrel (lettuce like herb)
Soufflé de Homard: lobster soufflé
Soufflé de Jambon: ham soufflé
Soufflé de Langouste: tiny lobster soufflé
Soufflé de Turbotin Florentine: turbot soufflé with wine cream, spinach & cheese sauce
Soufflé Glacé: iced soufflé
Soufflé Glacé à la Vanille: frozen vanilla mousse
Soufflé Glacé à l'Eau de Noix: frozen mousse with egg whites, puréed fruit, cream & nuts
Soufflé Glacé à l'Orange: soufflé with orange glaze
Soufflé Glacé au Cassis: black currant frozen mousse or soufflé
Soufflé Glacé au Chocolat: frozen chocolate mousse
Soufflé Glacé au Citron: frozen lemon mousse
Soufflé Glacé au Pernod: soufflé with Pernod (licorice flavored liqueur)
Soufflé Glacé aux Abricots: frozen apricot soufflé
Soufflé Glacé aux Fraises: frozen strawberry mousse
Soufflé Glacé aux Framboises: frozen raspberry soufflé
Soufflé Glacé aux Noisettes: frozen hazelnut mousse
Soufflé Glacé Praline: frozen soufflé with praline flavor (almond or hazelnut)
Soufflé Mirabelle: golden plum soufflé
Soufflé Rocambole: soufflé with mild garlic
Soufflé Rothschild: soufflé with pastry cream, eggs & Kirsch or brandied fruits
Soufflé Rothschild Grand Marnier: soufflé with pastry cream, glazed fruits, vanilla & Grand Marnier liqueur
Soufflé Stanhope: vanilla & chocolate soufflé with liqueured macaroons
Souillac Truffes Sous la Cendre: truffles cooked in ashes
Soumaintrain: strong soft cheese
Soupe à l'Ail Gratinée: soup with garlic, cheese & bread crumbs
Soupe à l'Oignon: onion soup
Soupe à l'Oseille: sorrel soup (lettuce like herb)
Soupe au Chou: cabbage soup
Soupe au Cresson: potato soup with nutmeg & watercress

Steak

Soupe au Pistou: soup with garlic, basil & herbs or soup of onions, tomatoes, green beans, dried beans, zucchini, potatoes, leeks, vermicelli & ground garlic, basil & herbs
Soupe aux Ecrevisses: crayfish (lobster) soup
Soupe aux Moules: mussel soup
Soupe aux Poissons: fish broth with grated Parmesan cheese & bread crusts rubbed with garlic
Soupe de Bouillabaisse: fish soup
Soupe d'Ecrevisses: creamed crayfish (lobster) soup
Soupe de Fruits au Champagne: cold fruit soup with champagne
Soupe de Moules: mussel soup
Soupe de Poissons: fish soup or thick fish soup with pasta
Soupe de Poissons Brestoise (Soir Seul): soup with fish caught near Brest — evenings only
Soupe de Poissons Marseillaise: fish soup from Marseilles
Soupe de Poissons Paimplaise: fish soup
Soupe de Tortue: turtle soup
Soupe Froide aux Fruits: cold fruit soup
Soupe Tortue au Xérès: turtle soup with sherry
Souvarov: small cakes with apricot jam
Spaghetti au Beurre: spaghetti with butter
Spaghetti aux Clovisses: spaghetti with clams
Spaghetti avec Sauce de Tomate ou à la Bolognaise: spaghetti with tomato or meat sauce
Spaghetti Napolitaine: spaghetti with tomato sauce & Parmesan cheese
Spécialités de la Maison: specialities of the house
Steak à la Moëlle: steak with poached marrow
Steak au Poivre: steak with pepper corns & flamed with cognac & heavy cream or pepper steak
Steak au Poivre Flambé à l'Armagnac: pepper steak flamed with cognac
Steak de Baudroie Poivre Vert: angler fish with green peppers
Steak de Canard au Cidre: duck steak in cider
Steak de Lotte au Calvados: fresh water angler fish in Calvados cider
Steak de Veau Choron: veal steak with artichoke bottoms, green peas, potatoes, tomato purée & sauce Choron (Béarnaise sauce with tomato purée)
Steak de Veau: veal steak
Steak de Veau Sauté Tessinoise: veal steak with Swiss cheese & buttered noodles

Steak

Steak en Chemise au Poivre Vert: batter fried steak with green peppers
Steak Frites: steak & French fries
Steak Haché Bercy: ground steak with sauce of white wine, butter, shallots, beef marrow & meat glaze
Steak Minute Pommes Soufflées: thin pounded steak with potato puffs
Steak Tartare: raw hamburger with egg & herbs on top (steak tartar)
St. Florentin: cream cheese
St. Honoré: pastry shell with gelatine egg custard & small cream puffs dipped in syrup & iced
St. Jacques Farcies à l'Oseille: scallops in the shell stuffed with sorrel (lettuce like herb)
St. Jacques Soubise: scallops in rice & onion cream sauce
St. Pierre Beurre Blanc: salt water fish with white butter wine sauce
St. Pierre (Sur Commande): salt water fish on special order
Suc: natural juice obtained from meats or vegetables
Succés: small cakes (petits fours)
Suc de Viande: juice from raw or cooked meat
Suédoise de Pommes: apple jelly
Sundae Fraise: strawberry sundae
Supplément Chantilly: whipped cream extra
Suprême de Barbue: brill (fish) in white sauce
Suprême de Barbue à l'Oseille: creamed filet of brill (fish) with sorrel (lettuce like herb)
Suprême de Barbue Bréval: brill (fish) in fish stock & butter
Suprême de Barbue Brévanne: brill (fish) in white sauce
Suprême de Canard Sauvage aux Nouilles Fraîches: breast & wings of duck with fresh noodles
Suprême de Caneton Lalonde: duck breasts in cream sauce
Suprême de Faisan: pheasant breast
Suprême de Féra: best slices of salmon-trout
Suprême de Féra au Vermouth: salmon-trout filets in vermouth
Suprême de Féra Pochés aux Herbes de Nos Alpes: poached salmon-trout in herbs
Suprême de Fruits: yeast cake with fruits & liqueur or brandy, apricot glaze & syrup
Suprême de Perche en Feuilleté au Beurre Blanc: slices of perch filet in puff pastry with white wine, herb & butter sauce
Suprême de Perdreau: partridge breast
Suprême de Pintadeau au Foie Gras: breasts of young

Tarte

Guinea fowl with goose or duck liver pâté
Suprême de Poularde Bâloise: fried or poached breast & wings of chicken
Suprême de Turbot au Cerfeuil: creamed turbot filets with chervil (herb)
Suprême de Turbot Cuba: turbot filets in white cream sauce
Suprême de Turbotin: filets of young turbot in white cream sauce
Suprême de Turbotin a l'Américaine: young turbot with white wine, brandy, lobster & fish cream sauce or cold mayonnaise, lobster & mustard or garnish of lobster tails & truffles
Suprême de Turbotin Soufflé: young turbot filet soufflé
Suprême de Volaille Truffé: chicken breast in white cream sauce with truffles
Suprêmes de Baudroie: angler fish filets in white cream sauce
Suprêmes de Volailles Maryland: chicken breasts & wings in casserole with cream gravy
Sur Commande: made to order or on demand
Table de Hors D'Oeuvres: appetizer table
Tablier de Sapeur: dish of fried tripe
Tagrine de Mouton: lamb stew with shaffron, white grapes & herbs
Talmouse: pastry tartlets with fillings & cheese base
Tapenade: tuna, garlic, anchovy & olive paste
Tartare: ground beef with raw egg yolks, anchovies, capers & Worcestershire sauce or tartar sauce
Tarte: cream tart with fruits
Tarte Alsacienne: apple tart
Tarte à l'Ananas: tart (pie) with pineapple & apricot glaze
Tarte à la Tomate: tomato tart
Tarte à l'Oignon: onion tart
Tarte au Citron: lemon custard tart
Tarte au Fromage: cheese tart
Tarte au Fromage Blanc: cream cheese cake with almonds & Kirsch
Tarte aux Abricots: apricot tart
Tarte aux Amandes: almond cream tart
Tarte aux Blettes: pie of greens & spinach beets
Tarte aux Cerises: cherry pie
Tarte aux Framboises: raspberry pie or tart
Tarte aux Fruits: fruit pie or tart
Tarte aux Groseilles: gooseberry tart
Tarte aux Mirabelles: tart with plums & sugar glaze with plum brandy

Tarte

Tarte aux Moules: mussels in pie
Tarte aux Myrtilles: huckleberry tart
Tarte aux Oranges: tart with orange & orange glaze
Tarte aux Pêches: peach tart with apricot glaze & raspberry brandy
Tarte aux Poires: pear tart on rice with milk, sugar, eggs & apricot or currant glaze
Tarte aux Pommes: apple pie
Tarte aux Pommes Chaudes: hot apple pie
Tarte aux Pommes des Demoiselles Tatin: apple pie
Tarte aux Prunes: custard tart with plum brandy & plums
Tarte Cassonade: brown sugar pie
Tarte Chaude: hot pie
Tarte Chaude aux Pommes: hot apple pie
Tarte du Jour: pie or tart of the day
Tarte Jamin: almond, Kirsch & lemon tart
Tartelette à l'Ananas: pineapple tart
Tartelette à la Rhubarbe: rhubarb tart
Tartelette à la Crème: tart with pastry cream
Tartelette au Caviar: pastry shell with caviar, mayonnaise & anchovies
Tartelette aux Cerises: cherry tart
Tartelette aux Fraises: strawberry tart
Tartelette aux Pêches: peach tart with currant or apricot syrup
Tartelette aux Pommes à la Normande: tart with vanilla rice, apples & apricot jam
Tartelette aux Tranches de Pommes: apple tart with pastry cream & apricot, cherry or strawberry glaze
Tartelette Frangipane: tartlet with frangipane (fruit) cream & almond paste
Tartelette Maison: homemade tarts
Tartelettes: tartlets
Tarte Maison: pie of the house
Tarte Meringuée: meringue tart
Tarte Normande: pie of eggs, dairy products & apples
Tarte Tatin: a pie or tart with carmelized apples
Tartine: bread with butter, jam, honey, etc.
Tende de Tranche: top round (cut of meat)
Tendron de Veau aux Nouilles Fraîches Truffé et Foie Gras: veal thorax cartilage with fresh noodles, truffles & goose liver pâté
Tendrons de Veau: the cartilage gristle of the thorax of veal
Terrine: cold molded coarsely ground meat pâté

Terrine

Terrine de Brochet et d'Anguille: pike and eel pâté
Terrine au Foie Gras: pâté of duck or goose liver
Terrine aux Foies de Volaille: chopped chicken liver pâté
Terrine aux Trois Poissons: pâté of three fish
Terrine de Bécasse: woodcock pâté
Terrine de Body: pâté of veal & bacon
Terrine de Brochet: pike pâté
Terrine de Brochet au Beurre Blanc: pike pâté with white butter sauce, wine, herbs, shallots & wine vinegar
Terrine de Brochet "Beurre Neige": pike pâté with whipped butter
Terrine de Caille Lucullus: quail pâté with stuffed truffles in sherry
Terrine de Cailles au Foie Gras: quail pâté with goose or duck liver pâté
Terrine de Campagne: pâté of mixed meats & livers
Terrine de Canard: ground duck pâté
Terrine de Canard aux Pistaches: pâté of forcemeat, duck livers & duck meat with pistachio nuts
Terrine de Canard du Chef: duck pâté of the chef
Terrine de Canard Truffée: duck pâté with truffles
Terrine de Chevreuil: deer pâté
Terrine d'Ecrevisses à la Cuillère (En Saison): crayfish (lobster) pâté (in season)
Terrine de Crustacés: shellfish pâté
Terrine de Faisan à la Gelée au Porto: pheasant pâté in port wine jelly
Terrine de Foie: liver pâté
Terrine de Foie de Canard Truffée: duck liver pâté with truffles
Terrine de Foie d'Oie en Gelée: goose liver pâté in meat jelly
Terrine de Foie Gras: chopped duck or goose liver pâté
Terrine de Foie Gras à la Gelée de Porto: chopped duck or goose liver pâté in port wine jelly
Terrine de Foie Gras Frais: fresh chopped duck or goose liver pâté
Terrine de Foie Gras Frais au Vieux Cognac: fresh chopped duck or goose liver pâté: with old cognac
Terrine de Foies de Volaille: chopped chicken liver paté
Terrine de Grives: thrush pâté
Terrine de Lapereau aux Noisettes: rabbit pâté with hazelnuts
Terrine de Lapin: rabbit pâté
Terrine de Lievre: rabbit pâté

Terrine

Terrine de Mer (En Saison): pâté of mixed seafoods (in season)
Terrine de Pâté Maison: pâté of the House
Terrine de Perche aux Ciboulettes: perch pâté with chives
Terrine of Pigeonneau Truffée et Pistachée: young pigeon pâté with truffles & pistachios
Terrine de Rascasse au Citron: hogfish pâté with lemon
Terrine de Rascasse aux Crevettes: hogfish & shrimp pâté
Terrine de Ris de Veau aux Noisettes: veal sweetbread pâté with hazelnuts
Terrine de St. Pierre à la Mousse de Tomate: fish pâté with tomato mousse
Terrine de Truite: trout pâté
Terrine de Veau au Port: veal pâté with port wine
Terrine de Volaille aux Noisettes: chicken pâté with hazelnuts
Terrine du Marin: seafood or fish pâté
Terrine Maison: house pâté
Terrine de Poisson: fish pâté
Terrine Pompadour: Pompadour style pâté
Terrine Ris de Veau: veal sweetbread pâté
Terrine St. Jacques Chaude: warmed moulded pâté of scallops
Terrine Trois Poissons: pâté of 3 fish
Terrinette de Foie Gras Strasbourgeoise: goose liver pâté
Tête de Porc: pig's head
Tête de Veau: boiled calf's head
Tête de Veau en Tortue: calf's head with dumplings, olives, truffles & veal tongue in wine sauce or calf's brains with tongue, eggs, cockscombs, Madeira wine & croutons
Tête de Veau Gribiche: jellied veal head with cold sauce (egg, oil, vinegar, gherkins, capers, parsley & strips of egg whites) OR calf's head with hard boiled eggs & tongue
Tête de Veau Ste. Ménéhould: calf's head with white wine sauce
Tête de Veau Vinaigrette: calf's head in vinaigrette sauce
Thon: tuna fish
Thon à la Grecque: tuna fish in bouillon with onions, garlic, carrots, olive oil & lemon juice
Thon à la Provençale: tuna fish filets with anchovy filets, onions, garlic, tomatoes, herbs & white wine
Thon à l'Huile: tuna fish in olive oil with lemon
Thon Frais (En Saison): fresh tuna fish in season
Thon Niçoise: tuna fish in white wine, tomatoes, garlic &

Tournedos

herbs
Tian Vençois: chard, spinach & zucchini in oil, bread crumbs, cheese, anchovies & sardines
Timbale: baked custard dessert
Timbale de Filets de Sole Valéry: individual dishes of filet of sole
Timbale de Fruits de Mer: flame proof dish with seafood
Timbale de Homard: lobster in timbale mould
Timbale d'Escargots au Chablis et Noisettes: mould dish with snails, hazelnuts & Chablis wine
Toast à la Moëlle: poached marrow on buttered toast
Toast aux Champignons: toast with mushrooms
Tomate Japonaise: stuffed tomato with mayonnaise, capers & salad greens
Tomates Antiboises: marinated tomatoes stuffed with tuna, hard boiled eggs, capers, parsley, herbs, mayonnaise & anchovy essence
Tomates Provençale: tomatoes with garlic bread
Tomme: semi hard cheese
Torteau Dresse: dish of seasoned crabmeat
Tortue: turtle
Tortue au Xérès: turtle soup with sherry
Tortue Clair: red turtle soup
Toulousain: beans, pork, goose, garlic & crumbs
Toulouse: pork sausage
Tournedos: steak filet or beef tenderloin tips
Tournedos à la Dauphinoise: filet of beef with mushrooms on toast with brown sauce
Tournedos à la Moëlle au Chinon: beef filet with marrow & red wine
Tournedos à la Strasbourgeoise: filet mignon with red cabbage strips & sausage with horseradish
Tournedos à l'Estragon: slices of beef filet with tarragon
Tournedos au Foie Gras: beef tenderloin tips with pâté
Tournedos au Poivre: tenderloin tips of beef with peppercorns
Tournedos au Poivre Vert: beef tenderloin tips with green pepper
Tournedos aux Cèpes: beef tenderloin tips with mushrooms
Tournedos aux Morilles à la Crème: beef tenderloin tips with creamed mushrooms
Tournedos de Charollais Rossini: beef tenderloin tips with pâté
Tournedos Flambé aux Morilles: flaming beef tenderloin tips

Tournedos

with mushrooms
Tournedos Flambé Médicis: flaming beef tenderloin tips, with artichoke bottoms, peas, carrots & turnips
Tournedos Forestière: beef tenderloin with mushrooms, bacon & potatoes or beef tenderloin tips with brown gravy, sherry & mushrooms
Tournedos Grillé: broiled beef tenderloin tips
Tournedos Henri IV: beef tenderloin tips with croutons & artichokes with Béarnaise sauce
Tournedos Masséna: beef tenderloin tips with artichoke bottoms, truffles, wine sauce & bone marrow
Tournedos Périgourdine Pommes: prime filet mignon with truffles & potatoes
Tournedos Rossini: beef tenderloin tips on crust with goose liver pâté, pan juices & Bordeaux wine
Tournedos Sauce Périgueux: filet of beef with brown sauce & truffles
Tournedos Vieux Strasbourg: beef tenderloin tips with pâté, red cabbage & sausage
Tourte: pastry tart, shell or pie
Tourteaux: king crab
Tourte de Bléa: tart with beets, pine nuts & currants
Tourte de Cailles: quail pie
Tourte de Caneton en Gelée: duckling & jelly in pastry shell
Tourte de Cuisses de Grenouilles: frog's legs in pastry shell
Tourte Glacée au Kirsch: pastry tart with Kirsch liqueur
Tourte Lorraine: pork & veal pie with eggs & seasoning
Tourterelle: turtle dove (bird)
Tourtière: puff pastry
Tranche: slice
Tranche de Poisson Rôti: slice of roast fish
Tranche Grasse: sirloin tip
Tranche Napolitaine: puff pastry with cream or whipped cream with powdered sugar or icing
Tranches de Saumon Fumé: slices of smoked salmon
Triomphe du Golfe: best fish in the Gulf
Tripes: intestines & chitterlings
Tripes à la Mode de Caen: tripe with calf's foot, carrots, leeks, herbs, garlic, spices & cider or tripes with kidneys, fat, white wine & calf's feet
Tripes Morvandelle: tripe with calf's feet, vegetables & white wine
Tripettes: sheep intestines in lard with tomatoes, herbs & seasonings

Truite

Tripous: lamb tripe with lamb's feet & veal intestines
Tripoux: mutton feet & veal offal stuffed with herbs & steamed potatoes
Tripoux Comme à l'Aurillac: veal tripe in casserole
Trogon: edible heart of vegetable
Tronçon de Selle d'Agneau Grillé: broiled saddle of lamb
Truffes: very rare underground wild mushrooms from Périgourd
Truffes à la Croque au Sel: raw truffles with salt
Truffes au Madère: truffles in Madeira wine
Truffes au Vin de Cahors: truffles with wine from Cahors
Truffes de Valéras en Brouillade: truffles with scrambled eggs
Truffes en Coffret: truffles in little case
Truffes en Croustade: truffles in pastry crust
Truffes en Feuilletage: truffles in puff pastry
Truffes Sous Cendre: charcoal broiled truffles
Truffes Sous la Cendre: charcoal broiled truffles
Truite: trout
Truite à l'Aligote Beurre Echalote: trout with shallot butter, creamed potatoes garlic & cheese
Truite au Beurre Blanc: trout in white wine broth & butter sauce
Truite au Bleu: live trout plunged into bouillon till the skin turns blue
Truite au Bleu Beurre Blanc Crème: freshly killed trout fried with white butter sauce
Truite au Bleu Meunière: freshly killed trout with lemon butter sauce
Truite au Champagne: trout in champagne
Truite au Château Châlon: trout with yellow wine
Truite au Lard: trout fried in bacon fat
Truite au Vermouth: trout in vermouth
Truite au Vin Rouge: trout in red wine
Truite aux Amandes: trout with almonds
Truite aux Noisettes: trout & hazelnuts
Truite Belle Meunière: fried trout with lemon & butter sauce
Truite Bovary au Champagne: trout in champagne
Truite Bouillie Sauce Verte: boiled trout with green sauce
Truite de l'Auberge à la Talleyrand: the inn's trout in chicken base, sherry cream sauce, carrots, onions & truffles
Truite de Lac: lake trout
Truite de Rivière à la Belle Meunière: river trout with lemon-herb butter sauce

Truite

Truite de Rivière aux Amandes: river trout with almonds
Truite de Rivière Court Bouillon: river trout in fish stock with spices
Truite de Rivière Grillée: broiled brook trout
Truite de Rivière Meunière: brook trout with lemon butter
Truite en Chemise: sautéed trout in crêpe
Truite en Gelée au Riesling: poached trout in white wine
Truite Farcie: stuffed trout
Truite Farcie aux Fines Herbes: trout stuffed with finely chopped herbs
Truite Farcie Braisée au Porto: stuffed trout with port wine
Truite Farcie en Chemise: boned trout stuffed with mousse
Truite Fourrée: stuffed trout
Truite Fumée: smoked trout
Truite Grillée aux Herbes: trout with herbs
Truite Meunière aux Amandes: trout in lemon butter with almonds
Truite Saumonée: salmon trout
Truite Sautée aux Amandes: trout fried in butter with almonds
Truite Soufflée: trout soufflé
Truite Soufflée au Chablis: trout soufflé with Chablis wine
Truite Soufflée au Tokay: trout soufflé with white wine
TToro: Basque fish stew
Tuiles: biscuits or cookies with vanilla, almonds & lemon
Tulipe de Pêche Grand Marnier: peach with Grand Marnier liqueur
Turban: rice mould with meat, fowl or fish
Turbot: turbot (sea bass)
Turbot à l'Estragon: turbot with tarragon
Turbot Amiral: boiled turbot with butter, anchovies, capers, chives & lemon sauce
Turbot au Coulis de Fenouil: turbot in fennel sauce (licorice flavored herb)
Turbot au Pouilly: turbot with white wine
Turbot aux Morilles: turbot with mushrooms
Turbot Beurre Blanc: turbot with sauce of whipped butter, vinegar & shallots
Turbot Braisé au Riesling: turbot braised in white wine
Turbot Dugléré: turbot in white wine, butter, shallots, parsley, tomatoes, cream & lemon juice
Turbot Flambé au Pernod: turbot flamed with Pernod (licorice flavored liqueur)
Turbot Grillé Beurre Blanc: broiled turbot with sauce of but-

Velouté

ter, shallots, wine & wine vinegar
Turbot Grillé Sauce Selon Désir: broiled trout with choice of sauce
Turbot Hollandaise: poached turbot with Hollandaise sauce OR turbot with egg yolk & cream sauce
Turbotin: small turbot
Turbotin au Coulis de Homard: young turbot with puréed lobster or lobster roe (eggs)
Turbotin du Golfe au Champagne: small gulf turbot in champagne
Turbotin Sauce Moutarde: small turbot with mustard sauce
Turbotin Soufflé: small turbot soufflé
Turbot Meunière: floured fried turbot with lemon & herb butter
Turbot Poché Hollandaise: poached turbot with Hollandaise sauce (egg yolk & cream sauce)
Turbot Poché ou Grillé: poached or grilled trout
Vacherin: soft cheese or meringues with whipped cream, soft fruit or cream
Vacherin Glacé: frosted meringues & whipped cream
Valencay: semi hard goat's milk cheese
Vapeur, à la: steamed
Veau: veal
Veau à la Berrichonne: veal stew with red wine & vegetables
Veau à la Flamande: veal with prunes
Veau à l'Estragon: veal with shallots & tarragon
Veau Chasseur: veal with mushrooms & tomatoes
Veau Farci, Garni de Champignons: veal breast stuffed with forcemeat of liver, mushrooms & wine with cream sauce
Veau Marengo: veal with onions & tomatoes
Veau Matelote: veal in red wine sauce
Veau Normande: veal with vegetables
Veau Prince Orloff: veal roast with onions & grated Swiss cheese
Veau Saumoné: veal marinated with herbs
Veau Sauté Chasseur: veal breast with shallots, mushrooms & wine
Veau Sylvie: veal roast stuffed with ham & Swiss cheese in brandy, Madeira wine & vegetables
Velouté: velvet sauce or soup
Velouté de Légumes: vegetable soup
Velouté d'Epinards: creamed chopped spinach
Velouté de Poisson: creamy fish soup
Velouté de Volaille: creamy chicken soup

Velouté

Velouté du Président Hereil: thick cream soup
Venaison: venison
Verte: herbed mayonnaise with spinach purée
Viande: meat
Viande de Grisons: dried beef
Viande Froide: cold meat
Viande Froide Mayonnaise: cold meat with mayonnaise
Viande Sechée des Grisons: dried beef
Vichyssoise: cold cream of leek & potato soup
Villeroy: white sauce with ham flavor
Vin: wine
Vinaigrette: sauce of oil, vinegar & herbs
Vin Blanc: white sauce with fish stock, cream, egg yolks & white wine
Vin Rosé: rosé wine
Vin Rouge: red wine
Voiture d'Entremets: pastry wagon
Volaille: poultry
Volaille à la Crème aux Cèpes: creamed chicken with mushrooms
Volaille à la Kieff (Kiev): balls of butter, chives, parsley in chicken breasts
Volaille de Bresse à la Crème: creamed Bresse chicken
Volaille de Bresse au Vin Rouge: Bresse chicken in red wine
Volaille de Bresse aux Morilles à la Crème: Bresse chicken with creamed mushrooms
Volaille de Bresse Braisée à l'Estragon: Bresse chicken braised with tarragon
Volaille de Bresse en Vessie: chicken from Bresse in bladder
Volaille de Bresse Rôtie: roast Bresse chicken
Volaille Demi Deuil: chicken with truffles, sauce suprême (white cream sauce) & rice
Volaille et Gibier: poultry & game
Volaille Truffée au Court-Bouillon: chicken in court-boullion with truffles
Vol au Vent: puff pastry shell with chopped foods in cream sauce
Vol au Vent aux Fruits: puff pastry shell with fruit
Vol au Vent d'Oeufs: puff pastry shell with hard boiled eggs in cream sauce
Vraie Limande: salt water fish
Xérès, à la: with sherry
Yaourt: Yogurt
Zephyr d'Ecrevisses: mousse with crayfish (lobster) & cream

Zingara

sauce
Zingara, à la: sauce for meat, fowl or eggs of meat stock, tomato purée, red pepper, Madeira wine, mushrooms, truffles, ham & ox tongue

Section II

MY FAVORITE FOODS

My Favorite Foods

In this section of the book, I have translated from English to French some of the common popular dishes you are accustomed to eating. Included will be the different French words for that particular dish.

Now if you have a strong urge for a specific food, you simply look it up in English, find the French expression and then look for it on your menu.

Naturally, this word on the menu will appear with other French words describing the sauce, garnish or preparation. You will then turn to the French section and look up the entire meaning of the dish. In this manner you are able to easily find that dish you are craving.

APPETIZERS — HORS D'OEUVRES

Chopped Chicken Livers: Pâté de Foies de Volaille
Cocktails:
   Grapefruit: Cocktail de Pamplemousse or Cocktail de Grapefruit
   Lobster: Cocktail de Homard or Cocktail d'Ecrevisses
   Seafood: Cocktail de Fruits de Mer
   Shrimp: Cocktail de Crevettes
Fruit Cup: Macédoine
Pâté: Pâté or Foie Gras

BEVERAGES — BOISSONS

Beer: Bière
Cider: Cidre
Coffee: Café
Juices:
   Apple: Jus de Pomme
   Orange: Jus d'Orange
   Tomato: Jus de Tomate
Milk: Lait
Tea: Thé
Water:
   Mineral: Eau Minérale
   Tap: Eau Naturale

Wine:
  Red: Vin Rouge
  Rosé: Vin Rosé
  White: Vin Blanc

DESSERTS — ENTREMETS

Cake: Gâteau
Chocolate Cake: Gâteau au Chocolat or Chocolatine
Cheese: Fromage
Cream Puffs: Profiteroles or Choux à la Crème
Custard, Caramel: Crème Caramel, Crème Renversée or Crème Renversée au Caramel
Ice Cream: Glace
  Chocolate: Glace au Chocolat or Glace Chocolat
  Strawberry: Glace aux Fraises or Glace Fraise
  Vanilla: Glace Vanille
  Banana Split: Banane Split
  Sundae: Coupe
  Strawberry: Coupe Glacé aux Fraises or Coupe aux Fraises
Pastries: Pâtisseries
  Apple Tart: Tarte aux Pommes
  Cheese Cake: Tarte au Fromage
  Cherry Tart: Tarte aux Cerises
  Fruit Tart: Tarte aux Fruits
Pudding, Chocolate: Pouding au Chocolat, Bavarois au Chocolat or Mousse au Chocolat
Sherbet: Sorbet
Whipped Cream: Chantilly or Crème Fouettée

EGGS — OEUFS

Baked: Oeufs au Four
Fried: Oeufs au Plat, Oeufs Plat Nature or Oeufs sur le Plat
Hard Boiled: Oeufs Durs
Poached: Oeufs Pôchés
Scrambled: Oeufs Brouillés
Soft Boiled: Oeufs à la Coque or Oeufs en Cocotte

FRUIT — FRUIT

Apples: Pommes
Apple Sauce: Compote de Pommes

Canteloupe: Melon
Cherries: Cerises
Date: Date
Fig: Figue
Fruit Cup: Macédoine or Macédoine de Fruits
Grapefruit: Pamplemousse or Grapefruit
Lemon: Citron
Lime: Citron Vert
Oranges: Oranges
Peaches: Pêches
Pears: Poires
Pineapple: Ananas
Plums: Prunes
Prunes: Pruneaux
Raspberries: Framboises
Strawberries: Fraises
Watermelon: Pastèque

MEATS and FOWL
VIANDES et VOLAILLE

BEEF — LAMB — PORK — POULTRY
BOEUF — AGNEAU — PORC — VOLAILLE

Bacon: Bacon, Lard or Poitrine
Baked Chicken: Poulet au Pot
Beef: Boeuf
Beef Short Ribs: Plat de Côtes de Boeuf or Côtes de Boeuf
Beefsteak: Biftec or Bifstec
Beef Tenderloin: Filet Mignon or Tournedos
Breaded Veal Cutlets: Escalope de Veau Panée or Escalope de Veau Viennoise
Broiled Chicken: Poulet Rôti or Poulet Grillé
Calf's Liver: Foie de Veau
Chicken: Poulet, Poularde, Coq, Coquelet or Poussin
Chicken Livers: Foies de Volaille
Duck: Canard or Caneton
Filet of Beef: Châteaubriand
Ham: Jambon
Lamb Chops: Côtes d'Agneau or Chops d'Agneau
Leg of Lamb: Gigot d'Agneau
Pepper Steak: Boeuf au Poivre or Steak au Poivre
Pork: Porc

Pork Chops: Côtes de Porc
Pork Cutlets: Escalope de Porc
Pork Sausage: Andouille or Cayettes
Pork Spareribs: Echines de Porc
Prime Ribs: Côtes de Porc
Rack of Lamb: Carré d'Agneau
Rib Steaks: Entrecôte de Boeuf
Roast Beef: Rôti de Boeuf
Roast Chicken: Poulet Rôti or Poulet Grillé
Sautéed Chicken: Poulet Sauté
Sirloin: Contre Filet, Aloyau de Boeuf or Entrecôte de Boeuf
Turkey: Dinde or Dindonneau
Veal: Veau
Veal Cutlet or Chop: Escalope de Veau or Côtes de Veau

OMELETTES — OMELETTES

Cheese: Omelette au Fromage
Ham: Omelette au Jambon
Herb: Omelette aux Fines Herbes
Mushroom: Omelette aux Morilles, Omelettes aux Champignons, Omelette aux Truffes, Omelette aux Girolles or Omelette de Périgord
Plain: Omelette Nature
Spanish: Omelette Espagnole

SALADS — SALADES

Chicken: Salade de Volaille
Cucumber: Salade de Concombres
Fruit: Salade de Fruits
Greens, Mixed: Salade Mixte
Lettuce: Salade Laitue or Salade Verte
Lobster: Salade de Homard, Salade de Langoustes or Salade d'Ecrevisses
Potato: Salade de Pommes or Pommes à l'Huile
Seafood: Salade de Poissons or Salade de Fruits de Mer
Shrimp: Salade de Crevettes
Tomato: Salade de Tomates
Tuna (Mayonnaise): Salade de Thon
Tuna (Niçoise) with tomatoes, anchovies, olives & vinaigrette dressing: Salade Niçoise

SEAFOOD & FISH — FRUITS DE MER & POISSONS

Clams: Palourdes
Crab: Crabe
Flounder: Filet or Carrelet
Halibut: Ftétan
Herring: Hareng
Lobster: Homard, Ecrevisse or Langouste
Mussels: Moules
Oysters: Huîtres, Belons or Portugaises
Pike: Brochet
Salmon: Saumon
Sardines: Sardines
Scallops: St. Jacques, Coquilles St. Jacques or Pétoncles
Shrimp: Crevettes or Scampis
Sole: Sole, Sole de Douvre or Filet de Sole
Stew: Bouillabaisse, Marmite Dieppoise or Ragoût de Fruits de Mer
Trout: Truite
Tuna: Thon
Turbot: Turbot

SOUPS — SOUPES

Chicken: Consommé Adèle
Chicken Broth: Consommé de Volaille
Chicken, Cream of: Crème de Volaille
Fish: Soupe de Poissons or Bouillabaisse
Fish, Cream of: Crème de Poissons
Onion: Soupe à l'Oignon
Pea: Crème de Pois
Tomato: Crème de Tomate or Chagrillan
Vegetable: Potage de Légumes, Potage Bonne Femme or Brunoise

VEGETABLES — LEGUMES

Artichoke Bottoms: Fonds d'Artichauts
Artichoke Hearts: Coeurs d'Artichauts
Asparagus: Asperges
Beans, Green: Haricots Verts
Broccoli: Brocoli

Brussels Sprouts: Choux de Bruxelles
Cabbage: Chou
Carrots: Carottes
Cauliflower: Choufleur
Celery: Céleri
Eggplant: Aubergine
Mushrooms: Champignons, Morilles, Girolles or Truffes
Onion: Oignon
Onion Rings: Oignons Frits à la Française
Peas: Pois or Petits Pois
Peppers, Green: Poivre Vert
Potatoes, Baked: Pomme de Terre au Four or Pomme au Four
Potatoes, Boiled: Pommes de Terre à l'Anglaise or Pommes Anglaises
Potatoes, French Fried: Pommes de Terre Frites, Pommes Frites or Frites
Potatoes, Mashed: Pommes de Terre Soufflées, Pommes Mousseline, Mousseline or Purée
Potatoes, Sautéed: Pommes de Terre Sautées or Pommes Sautées
Sauerkraut: Choucroute
Spinach: Epinards
Tomato: Tomate

MISCELLANEOUS

Bill: l'Addition
Bread: Pain
Breakfast: Le Petit Déjeuner
Butter: Beurre
Cream: Crème
Dinner: Le Dîner
Drink Included in Menu Prices: Boisson Compris
Drink Not Included in Menu Prices: Boisson Non Compris
Honey: Miel
Horseradish: Raifort
Ice: Glaçons
Jam, Jelly: Confiture
  Cherry: Confiture de Cerises
  Marmelade: Marmelade
  Strawberry: Confiture de Fraises
Lunch: Le Déjeuner
Mustard: Moutarde

Nuts: Noix
  Cashew: Noix d'Acajou
  Chestnut: Marron
  Hazelnut: Noisette
  Peanut: Cacahuète
  Walnut: Noix
Pepper: Poivre
Salt: Sel
Sandwich: Sandwich
  Grilled Ham & Cheese: Croque Monsieur
  Grilled Chicken & Cheese: Croque Madame
  Grilled Cheese & Tomato: Croque Fromage et Tomate
Sugar: Sucre
Tip Included in Menu Prices: Service Compris
Tip Not Included in Menu Prices: Service Non Compris
Waffle: Gaufre
Water: Eau
  Mineral: Eau Minérale
  Tap: Eau Naturale

HELPFUL HINTS

Here are some extra expressions to make your dining a more pleasurable experience.

In French, the word **MENU** means the fixed price fare of the restaurant. If you want a menu, ask for **La carte, s'il vous plait.** When you want your check, **L'addition s'il vous plait.** If you want to divide a meal, which is very acceptable, **Pour partager, s'il vous plait.**

Couvert is the cover charge for bread, butter & table setting
Compris Service means tips & taxes are included in the menu prices
Tout Compris again means all tips & taxes are included in the menu prices
Boisson Compris means a drink is included in the menu prices
Boisson Non Compris means your drink is not included in the menu prices
Non Compris or **Service Non Compris** means the tips & taxes are not included in the menu prices
En Sus is an extra charge for whatever item is listed in front of these words
S.G. means the price is dependent on the current market price of the item
Prix Fixe is the price of a complete meal, including drink & dessert
Plat du Jour is the dish of the day
Garni means the dish comes with a salad or vegetable

Section III

MY FAVORITE RESTAURANTS

My Favorite French Restaurants

CANADA
Montreal
  Auberge St. Tropez
  Café Martin
  Chez Bardet
  La Popina
  La St. Amable
  Le Cafe de Paris
  Le Castillion

FRANCE
Avignon
  Hiely
  La Fourchette
Beaune
  De Chambertin
  La Rotisserie
Biarritz
  Chez Albert
Bordeaux
  Aquitania
Cannes
  La Bonne Auberge
  Le Pompon Rouge
Mougins
  Le Moulin de Mougins
Nice
  La Poularde Chez Lucullus
  St. Moritz
Paris
  Allard
  Au Quai D' Orsay
  Brasserie Flo
  Chez Edgard
  La Coupole
  La Tour D'Argent

FRANCE
- Paris (continued)
    - Lasserre
    - Le Pactole
    - Le Petit Zinc
    - Lipp
    - Prunier
    - Vivarios
- St. Tropez
    - Fifine
- Tours
    - Barrier

HONG KONG
- Gaddi's

UNITED STATES

ARIZONA
- Scottsdale
    - Chez Louis
    - Etienne

CALIFORNIA
- San Francisco
    - Alexis
    - La Bourgogne
    - La Mirabelle

FLORIDA
- Boca Raton
    - Le Vielle Maison
- Ft. Lauderdale
    - Le Cordon Bleu
- Miami
    - Cafe Chauveron
    - Chalet Gourmet
    - La Boheme
    - Le Festival
- Palm Beach
    - Petit Marmite

ILLINOIS
  Chicago
    Café La Tour
    Jacques
MARYLAND
  Baltimore
    Circle One
MASSACHUSETTS
  Boston
    Joseph's
NEW YORK
  Manhattan
    La Caravelle
    La Grenouille
    Le Cirque
    Le Moal
    Le Perigord-Park
    Lutece
    Steak Pommes Frites
OHIO
  Cleveland
    Wagonwheel
TEXAS
  Houston
    Maxim's
  San Antonio
    La Louisiane
UTAH
  Salt Lake City
    La Fleur De Lys

Approximate Conversion Table
Based on 4.6 Francs = One Dollar

Francs		Dollars
1	=	$ .22
2	=	.44
3	=	.66
4	=	.88
5	=	1.10
6	=	1.32
7	=	1.54
8	=	1.76
9	=	1.98
10	=	2.20
11	=	2.42
12	=	2.64
13	=	2.86
14	=	3.08
15	=	3.30
16	=	3.52
17	=	3.74
18	=	3.96
19	=	4.18
20	=	4.40
25	=	5.50
30	=	6.60
35	=	7.70
40	=	8.80
45	=	9.90
50	=	11.00

NOTES

NOTES

NOTES

NOTES

Al Ellison's other Menu Readers are available from your bookseller or from Ellison Enterprises.

When ordering add 50¢ postage and handling per book. Make checks payable to Ellison Enterprises.

To: Ellison Enterprises
   1919 Purdy Ave.
   Miami Beach, Fla. 33139

   Please send me:

Quantity	Each book $2.95	Price
	Ellison's French Menu Reader	
	Ellison's Spanish Menu Reader	
	Ellison's Italian Menu Reader	
	Ellison's German Menu Reader	
	Ellison's Mexican Menu Reader	
	Ellison's Latin American Menu Reader	
	Ellison's Portuguese Menu Reader	
	Ellison's Swiss Menu Reader	
	Postage	
	Florida Sales tax, if applicable	
	Total	

NAME _____
STREET _____
CITY _____ STATE _____ ZIP _____